SECRETS
OF WINNING
LOTTO &
LOTTERY

STRATEGY TOOLS TO WIN MILLIONS OF DOLLARS!

AVERY CARDOZA

SECRETS
OF WINNING
LOTTO &
LOTTERY

STRATEGY TOOLS TO WIN MILLIONS OF DOLLARS!

AVERY CARDOZA

CARDOZA PUBLISHING

Cardoza Publishing is the foremost gaming and gambling publisher in the world with a library of almost 200 up-to-date and easy-to-read books and strategies. These authoritative works are written by the top experts in their fields and with more than 10 million books in print, represent the best-selling and most popular gaming books anywhere.

FIRST EDITION

Library of Congress Catalog Number: 2016940179
ISBN 10: 1-58042-333-7   ISBN 13: 978-1-58042-333-5

Visit our new web site (www.cardozabooks.com) or write us for a full list of books, advanced and computer strategies.

CARDOZA PUBLISHING

P.O. Box 98115, Las Vegas, NV 89193
Toll Free Phone (800)577-WINS
email: cardozabooks@aol.com
www.cardozabooks.com

ABOUT THE AUTHOR

Avery Cardoza, the world's foremost authority on gambling and a million-selling author of more than 40 books and advanced strategies, is the founder of Cardoza Publishing (publisher of more than 200 gaming titles, 10 million copies sold) and owner of the legendary Gambler's Book Club and iconic Gambler's General Store in Las Vegas. Millions of gamblers have learned how to play and win money at gambling following his no-nonsense practical advice.

Cardoza has been studying numbers and winning systems since he was five-years old. He has developed the most powerful lottery software and strategies ever formulated including the only systems using powerful Level II keys such as kings, wizards, and courts, and Level III advanced strategies found nowhere else. Cardoza is one of the foremost experts on predictive randomness for lotteries, the heart and soul of strategies that have won players millions upon millions of dollars. His work on lotto and lottery strategies includes the powerful *Lottery Super System*, the "bible" on beating lotto and lottery, *Secrets of Winning Lotto & Lottery*, and more than a dozen specialized Level III advanced strategies.

Cardoza's work is the centerpiece of LotterySuperSystem.com, the powerful online site for casual and serious players looking to win millions of dollars at lotto and lottery games.

TABLE OF CONTENTS

1
INTRODUCTION

I'm going to show you how to use my exclusive strategies to increase your chances of making millions of dollars playing lotto and lottery games!

Millions of people play the lottery every week, but most do so aimlessly, picking birthdays, anniversaries and other random numbers and dates. And just about every one of them is a consistent loser. Let me ask you a question: Are you tired of being one of those players who throws away money week by week with almost nothing to show for it? Are you fed up with randomly picking numbers with no rhyme or reason other than feelings, hunches or anniversaries of one sort or another? If the answer is yes—good! This book is going to change that.

I'm going to give you the tools to beat any lotto and lottery game in every U.S. state, Canadian province, and worldwide jurisdiction. All my strategies are aimed at shooting for the jackpot and gathering small wins to add to your coffers along the way. It isn't easy to win money playing lottery games, but the fact is that millions of people win prizes every week. Some win a few dollars, some win thousands or even a million dollars, and a lucky few win hundreds of millions of dollars.

In this book I'm going to reveal the most important secret that every successful lottery player must know to increase his or her odds of winning jackpots. You're going to learn the important and very powerful core strategies (also called Level I strategies), the foundation of all winning strategies.

Read on! You'll be one step closer to winning the jackpot of your dreams!

2

THE THEORY OF WINNING

There are patterns that are clearly discernible when you study a history of past lotto and lottery results. You'll see streaks of certain numbers or groups of numbers repeating more often than mathematical averages would suggest while other numbers that rarely get drawn suddenly come on in a flourish. If you were able to predict these patterns, you would do very well in lotto and lottery games. In fact, you'd get rich.

But can you predict these patterns based on past results?

From one point of view, no, past results of random events do not influence future results. But from a different perspective, past results do have meaning. Why did one number get picked six out of 10 games and another seven out of 10 games? And several other numbers didn't appear even a single time? Those occurrences were real and they *did* happen. But why?

That is not an easy question to answer. Let's step back a second and reexamine the word "random" as it applies to lottery balls. One fact is indisputable: No two items are alike. Not two people—and no, identical twins are not really identical—not two raindrops, nor even any of the balls used for lottery games. They may look similar, they may feel similar, and indeed they are similar.

But they are not the same.

Put those balls under a microscope and you will see variances in material density and in patterns on the surface, especially after steady use wears the balls unevenly.

Heck, if nothing else, every number printed on the balls carries a varying degree of paint to mark the digits. The number 8 uses less paint than the 18 and more paint than the 9. If you collected 10 balls with the number 8 affixed to them and examined them with your naked eye, they would appear identical, but they would be anything but under the fine eye of the microscope. Dissect these balls and you will find a further wealth of dissimilarities, so much so that you wouldn't even dare to suggest they were identical.

But do the physical differences affect their chances of coming out of the chute? They sure do! The real question is whether those differences affect their chances *enough* to predict future drawings based on the observations of past drawings.

When physical devices are in play, there will be a **bias**, a tendency of certain results to occur in greater frequency than pure randomness would suggest. The actual results would be influenced by all the forces in play—such as the device, the temperature, the many physical properties and characteristics of the ball being set in motion, and the person activating the event. There just has to be *enough* of a bias to make your plays worthwhile.

So we circle back to the question: Can you beat lotto and lottery games based on recent past results? Mathematically, in a coin flip, it is a fact that past results don't affect the chances of future flips landing heads or tails, nor of some lottery or lotto balls coming up more frequently than others—if all else is equal. *If all else is equal.* But as we discussed above, not all else is equal.

Throw everything else we talked about out the window for a moment and let's go back to a simple fact: When you study past drawings, there are distinct patterns that have occurred.

Some numbers came up more frequently than the math would predict, and some numbers appeared less frequently. In roulette, which also relies on physical devices to determine winners, astute players through the years have made a fortune studying past results on badly biased wheels and using those findings to kill casinos until management got wise to the bias and stopped the game.

Doubters can talk all they want about math and expectations and percentages, but anyone can see that some numbers have performed better than other numbers in a series of drawings while some have fared worse. In a lotto game, a particular set of six numbers will get drawn. The reason for these six particular numbers getting drawn at that very moment? Who knows. *Some numbers have to be drawn.* When a new drawing takes place, why those particular six numbers are drawn is a mystery no mathematician or fortune teller on earth can answer.

But once a series of balls is drawn, and another series, and then another gets drawn as well, there are very real patterns and trends that occurred, whether anyone can explain that reason or not.

In games or events where chance is involved, you can often calculate the likelihood that an event will occur—such as heads or tails on a coin, the number 32 being spun in roulette, a pair of aces getting dealt in hold'em, the chances of a 16 getting busted by the dealer in blackjack—but you could not predict with 100% accuracy the actuality of that event occurring.

While there are mathematical facts to be considered, there is also unpredictability and the unknown in many situations— and there is bias.

In any game where physical properties are involved, like lottery drawings or roulette, bias is a factor that must be considered. You don't need to be able to identify the reason for an actual bias or why something happened —at the end of the day, knowledge of the causation is irrelevant. You just need to know *what* happened. And might happen again.

So then, you ask, how can you discover a bias?

Simple. You just need to track the numbers and patterns that have emerged in a recent history of drawings. The results will be plain as day.

For this group of people, the observers that say you cannot ignore what you see with your own eyes and that the results are real—which indeed they are if they have occurred—a wealth of strategies is available to beat lotto and lottery games.

3
DIFFERENCES BETWEEN LOTTO & LOTTERY

While lotto games are technically considered a type of lottery game, in general usage there are differences between the two, and I explain these below.

1. In lotto, numbers are drawn from only one container, while numbers in the lottery come from separate containers.

2. In lotto, there are no duplications of numbers. For example, in a 39-ball lotto game, exactly 39 balls numbered 1 through 39 are in the container. So if the first ball drawn is 12, it cannot be drawn again since it has already been removed. In lottery, each container has 10 balls, numbered 0 through 9, and each ball drawn could duplicate other balls already drawn in the other tubes since they are independent events. It is not unusual to see lottery games with two or more duplicate numbers. For example, a draw could be 9-9-7, 0-5-0, or even 4-4-4.

3. In lotto, the order in which balls are drawn is irrelevant to your winning results, while in a lottery, the order of balls drawn is the difference between winning and losing. For example, if the balls drawn in a six-ball lotto game are 11, 33, 5, 7, 36 and 20, you win if enough of your numbers are drawn regardless of the order in which you picked them or in which way they are displayed. Newspapers and websites often display the numbers in ascending order, so those winning numbers might be displayed as 5, 7, 11, 20, 33, 36.

In a four-ball lottery, if the numbers drawn are 9-0-3-3, having the numbers reversed to 3-3-0-9 or scrambled, as in

3-0-9-3, does you no good. Only the sequence 9-0-3-3 is a winner. (Note: Some lottery games offer additional bets that allow you to cover your numbers in other combinations, but they are additional bets—really separate tickets but with the convenience of placing the numbers on one ticket—that require more money to play.

If a six-ball lottery game requires at least four of the numbers to be chosen, and you have those four numbers, you have a winner, though of course you would rather have five of the six for an even bigger prize—or all six for the jackpot!

4. In lottery games, the payoffs remain consistent. Most lottery games cost just $1 to play. Winning a Pick 3 lottery typically nets $500 in prizes while a Pick 4 might bring in $5,000. These payoffs will be posted so that you know what you're getting into before you buy your ticket. On the other hand, the jackpot in lotto games varies widely and could be huge one week and even bigger the following week. You don't know what you can win until the drawing because the jackpot grows as more people buy tickets.

4

CHOSEN NUMBERS & REGRESSION LEVELS

CHOSEN NUMBERS

Chosen numbers are the numbers you have identified through analysis methods or through sheer randomness to play in a lotto or lottery game. You feel these are the most *important numbers* to put on your tickets, which is why you will use them as part of your potential winning tickets. So yes, you can think of chosen numbers as important numbers because, well, they are. These are the very numbers where you will be putting your money, betting that they can go all the way and hit a jackpot for you.

Before you read this book, your chosen numbers probably consisted of, for lack of any better plan, randomly picked numbers with no rhyme or reason other than feelings, hunches, birthdays, anniversaries or what-the-heck types of choices. Maybe you took numbers off your driver's license.

But if you follow the advice in this book, that is going to change.

The main focus of this book, besides educating you in the important periphery topics necessary to a winning approach— such as money management and other practical matters—is to identify the top performing numbers in various analyses you will choose to beat lotto and lottery games. In other words, by using the core strategies you will learn here.

If you're seeking to play only one ticket per game, you only need as many chosen numbers as the number of balls that will get drawn. For example, in a four-ball lottery, you only need four chosen tickets, and in a six-ball lotto game, you would work with six chosen numbers. Most players, however, choose to attack the games with a bank of tickets to increase their chances of winning, perhaps playing five or 10 tickets per drawing. These players would need more than the minimum number of chosen numbers to play their tickets.

Indeed, their problem is often that they have many more numbers than they can play on a single ticket. For example, your core strategies might identify 10 numbers to play. But if you're playing a six-ball game, you can't get all your numbers in play on a single ticket, nor can you cover all possible combinations by playing even five or 10 tickets. In fact, to cover every combination of those 10 numbers would require you to play 924 tickets! A $924 investment in a single lotto game is not only crazy or foolish, depending upon your situation and point of view, but it is a much bigger investment than the $5 or even the $10 you want to play.

But no worries—you can cover all your numbers with just a few tickets by using wheeling systems. We'll look at wheeling systems later, but first we'd better get around to figuring out how to find the best numbers to play and the core strategies you will use to go after jackpots.

REGRESSION ANALYSIS

One important consideration in all the core strategies you will learn is how deep a game history to use when forming your analyses. Determining the depth level of an analysis, that is, the number of games you would chart to determine patterns, is called a **regression analysis**. Regression analysis is a fancy term for keeping a history of the numbers that have been drawn in past games. The purpose of a regression analysis is to help you detect patterns. The regression level of an analysis refers to the number of prior games you decide to chart. How deep a game history to use when forming your analyses is an important consideration in all the core strategies you will learn in this book.

A regression analysis charts the raw data from a specified number of prior lottery or lotto drawings (the regression level), such as 25 or 100 games, to determine the number of times an event has occurred. In these instances, the regression levels would be 25 and 100 games, respectively. You could choose other regression levels, for example 50 games or 250 games, depending on your philosophical approach or the dictates of the particular strategy you're playing. Various strategies require deep levels of regression while others might require as few as five or 10 drawings.

The depth of a regression analysis is an important consideration in your core strategies. And if you decide to move forward to advanced Level II and Level III strategies, it is essential. Very advanced strategies call for particular regression levels, sometimes combining varying penetration depths to identify streaks and patterns. These Level II and Level III strategies are beyond the scope of this book, but the powerful Level I core strategies covered here are the basis of these advanced plays so it is important that you learn them—not just to have a powerful attack now, but as a foundation if you decide to move to the next level.

THREE & FOUR BALL LOTTERY

THE BASICS OF PLAY

Three-ball and four-ball lottery games are offered throughout the country in almost all states and are extremely popular. They are easy to play and offer fast results and big prizes.

There are three separate containers in three-ball lottery games and four separate containers in four-ball lottery games, with each container filled with 10 balls numbered 0 through 9. A ball will be drawn from each container, in order, until all the balls for the game have been drawn; that is, three balls in the three-ball game and four balls in the four-ball game. Thus, you might see the numbers 5-7-2 drawn in a three-ball game, and 9-1-3-3 drawn in a four-ball game.

The winning tickets would match these numbers: 5-7-2 and 9-1-3-3 in the three-ball and four-ball games, respectively. If your three-ball ticket reads 5-7-2, you would be a winner. If your ticket reads 2-5-7, however, you would not be a winner— the ticket would be a loser, even though you hold the correct three digits. In traditional lottery games, the order in which numbers are drawn counts for everything because payouts are not for three correctly chosen numbers in a random sequence, they are for three correctly chosen numbers *in the exact order* in which they were drawn.

Note that in the earlier four-ball draw of 9-1-3-3, the number 3 was repeated twice. That is possible in lottery because each number is drawn from a different container with balls numbered 0 through 9. It could even be drawn three times, or four times in a four-ball game, as in 3-3-3-3. (In lotto games, however, that is not possible since there are no duplicate numbers in the bins. Once a 3 is drawn, another 3 cannot be pulled for that drawing. The other five balls drawn would comprise some combination of the remaining numbers in the bin.)

Box and Combination Bets

Some states feature additional bets that allow you to win in more ways than simply picking the winning number in the *exact order* drawn, known as a **straight bet**. In states offering these additional options, you can also *box* your numbers, known as a **box bet**, and have the three numbers appear in any order. Or you can play a **straight/box bet**, where you win if the ticket comes in exactly as you picked or if it comes in any order, which is actually a two-ticket play. Or you can play a **combination bet**, which is actually a six-ticket bet since you are playing all six combinations possible (of a particular three numbers) in the three-ball game.

STRATEGY OVERVIEW

When you chart numbers in lottery games, you don't blindly list the digits drawn. It would take close to 1,000 daily drawings in three-ball lottery games—combinations of 0-0-0 all the way to 9-9-9—if each combination were to be drawn exactly once before a repeated combination occurred.

In reality many combinations would repeat two times, three times and even more before other numbers occurred on even a single occasion. You would likely wait more than three years of daily drawings before every single combination occurred at least once.

That would give you nothing to work with and you couldn't form a useful strategy with a combination pool that vast. You'd never get anywhere.

Charting full numbers would make no sense anyway because each digit in a three- or four-ball lottery is drawn from its own pool and is independent of other digits being drawn. Charting numbers as a whole would ignore the fact that a number drawn from the first pool has nothing to do with a number drawn from a second, third or even fourth pool.

The proper way to analyze the lottery is by charting each pool of balls separately. Let's go back to our three-ball example. The winning combination of 5-7-2 reveals the results of three separate drawings. In the first pool, or position, the number 5 was selected from the pool of 10 balls, numbered from 0-9 (0-1-2-3-4-5-6-7-8-9). In the second pool, the number 7 was selected. Note that this pool, as well as the pool in the third ball, in which a 2 was drawn, contains an entirely separate set of 10 balls numbered 0-9.

So, these three separate pools of numbers gave you a final drawing of 5-7-2. If this were four-ball lottery, an additional ball would be drawn and you would have one more digit as part of the combination.

Since there are three separate drawings, you chart each set individually. To properly track these numbers, you create a worksheet with three columns, one for each number drawn. In other words, you track each combination by running a *positional analysis* of the individual digits. Let's look at that now.

POSITIONAL ANALYSIS

Positional analysis is the science of charting and statistically identifying and analyzing balls by position from a specified number of games in which each ball gets drawn from a different bin, such as happens in three-ball and four-ball lottery games. Your analysis will track these results and parse the information so that you can run further analyses from this data; for example, numbers that were most frequently drawn and numbers that were least frequently drawn.

Let's say that the previous 10 drawings were as follows:

$$1\text{-}7\text{-}3$$
$$1\text{-}9\text{-}0$$
$$0\text{-}7\text{-}6$$
$$3\text{-}1\text{-}7$$
$$8\text{-}0\text{-}7$$
$$9\text{-}9\text{-}0$$
$$8\text{-}7\text{-}4$$
$$3\text{-}4\text{-}6$$
$$2\text{-}2\text{-}9$$
$$1\text{-}0\text{-}5$$

The number of each ball drawn is separated by a dash to indicate its standing as an individual number. Once individual drawings are separated and identified by digits, it's a lot easier to manage the data and work with predictive analysis.

You'll start by creating a *Positional Drawing History*.

A **Positional Drawing History** is a chart that lists the date and the balls selected for each drawing, by position, for a specified number of drawings. It organizes lottery drawings in an easy-to-see format so that you can easily track patterns, trends and unusual activity.

Below is a Positional Drawing History of a three-ball lottery game. You'll see that in addition to a column showing the date of the drawing, there is a column for each of the three balls.

POSITIONAL DRAWING HISTORY
Three-Ball Lottery / 10 Games

Date	Position		
	1	2	3
3/7	1	7	3
3/8	1	9	0
3/9	0	7	6
3/10	3	1	7
3/11	8	0	7
3/12	9	9	0
3/13	8	7	4
3/14	3	4	6
3/15	2	2	9
3/16	1	0	5

Each horizontal row represents a three-ball drawing on the date indicated, and the columns chart the ball drawn in each of the three positions. Position 1 shows the first ball drawn, Position 2 shows the second ball drawn, and Position 3 shows the third and last ball drawn.

Following is a Positional Drawing History for a four-ball lottery game. It is exactly the same as the three-ball Positional Drawing History chart except that there is an additional column to chart the fourth ball.

POSITIONAL DRAWING HISTORY
Four-Ball Lottery / 10 Games

	Position			
Date	**1**	**2**	**3**	**4**
9/1	9	4	4	1
9/2	2	0	2	7
9/3	9	7	5	7
9/4	6	4	7	0
9/5	5	9	3	3
9/6	8	3	7	7
9/7	4	9	6	2
9/8	2	2	3	8
9/9	9	8	6	9
9/10	1	9	2	2

Each horizontal row represents a four-ball drawing on the date indicated, and the columns chart the ball drawn in each of the four positions. Position 1 shows the first ball drawn, Position 2 shows the second ball drawn, Position 3 shows the third ball drawn, and Position 4 shows the fourth and last ball drawn.

But to understand the frequency of occurrence for a large number of drawings, or even for a short range, you need a chart specifically set up for this purpose, a *Positional Analysis Raw Chart*.

Positional Analysis Raw Chart

A **Positional Analysis Raw Chart** keeps track of the *frequency* of drawn numbers for each digit in a lottery over a specified number of games. The matrix lists 10 numbers vertically, 0 through 9, one row for each of the balls in a lottery, and then the numbers 1, 2, 3 and 4 going across, these columns representing each of the four positions from which the balls were drawn in a four-ball lottery. (A three-ball lottery would only have three numbers going across.)

Each time a ball is drawn, you mark a dot in the appropriate area in the matrix. If the numbers drawn were 9-4-4-1, you would put a dot in the row corresponding to the number 9 and in the column marked 1 representing the first ball drawn. Similarly, you would insert a dot in the second row horizontal to the number 4 and in the column marked 2, plus a dot in the third column horizontal to the number 4, and a dot in the fourth column horizontal to the number 1.

Here is how your chart would look after this first draw.

POSITIONAL ANALYSIS RAW CHART
Four-Ball Lottery / 1 Drawings

	1	2	3	4
0				
1			•	
2				
3				
4		•	•	
5				
6				
7				
8				
9	•			

After 10 drawings your chart begins to fill.

POSITIONAL ANALYSIS RAW CHART
Four-Ball Lottery / 1 Drawings

	1	2	3	4
0		•		•
1	•			•
2	••	•	••	••
3		•	••	•
4	•	••	•	
5	•		•	
6	•		••	
7		•	••	•••
8	•	•		•
9	•••	•••		•

You can observe patterns forming in each of the four columns. Some numbers in the first column appeared more often than others in that column, and some less often. In a small sample such as this, you'll also see numbers that didn't appear on even a single occasion in a column. There are real trends to take note of in these 10 lottery games and they are easily analyzed when you create a Positional Analysis Raw Chart.

But to make this information easier to use—in other words, not just a bunch of dots—you convert the dots into numbers so that, at a glance, you can easily see the top performers. This next chart, which refines the data from the dots in a Positional Analysis Raw Chart into a more human-readable format, is called a **Positional Analysis Refined Chart**.

As you can see, analyzing charts in number form, as opposed to dots, is much easier to do.

POSITIONAL ANALYSIS REFINED CHART
4-Ball Lottery / 10 Drawings

	1	2	3	4
0		1		1
1	1			1
2	2	1	2	2
3		1	2	1
4	1	2	1	
5	1		1	
6	1		2	
7		1	2	3
8	1	1		1
9	3	3		1

This chart shows just 10 games. Let's say you're tracking 100 games. The numbers might look like this after they have been converted into a Positional Analysis Refined chart:

POSITIONAL ANALYSIS REFINED CHART
4-Ball Lottery / 100 Drawings

	1	2	3	4
0	9	18	15	7
1	16	9	7	13
2	5	12	14	14
3	14	7	11	6
4	8	11	4	13
5	4	7	9	10
6	8	8	6	11
7	10	10	13	7
8	15	13	11	11
9	11	5	10	8

The Positional Analysis Refined Chart is still raw data that needs one more refinement to extract the essential information you will use as the centerpiece of your strategies. How you refine these numbers determines the results you'll get. The most important of these refinements are a Best Number Analysis and an Overdue Number Analysis.

It is time to fire up the powerful core strategies you're going to use to predict future results!

CORE STRATEGY #1:
BEST NUMBER ANALYSIS

The core analyses are seeking to identify the top performing numbers over a specified number of drawings and the most important, or at least the most used core analytical tool is a *Best Number Analysis*. A **Best Number Analysis** organizes results of the Positional Analysis Refined Chart with the specific purpose of identifying numbers that have been the most frequently drawn, by position, over a specified number of games.

The Best Number Analysis sorts the raw information by frequency of occurrence in each of the three or four positions (separate pools from which the balls are drawn) so that you can easily see the top performing numbers. For example, you might run a best number analysis with a regression level of 35 games, 100 games, or perhaps even 250 games.

This next chart shows the first 10 games of the four-ball lottery we had tracked earlier. You can see early patterns developing. In Positions 1 and 2, number 9 led all balls with three appearacnes each, while in Position 3, four balls—2, 3, 6 and 7 were tied with two appearances each. In Position 4, number 7 had the early lead with three appearances.

As you get more drawings entered into the worksheet, frequency of appearances at the top (and bottom) tend to separate more.

BEST NUMBER ANALYSIS
Four-Ball Lottery / 10 Drawings

Position 1		Position 2		Position 3		Position 4		Best Numbers
#	**Frq**	**#**	**Frq**	**#**	**Frq**	**#**	**Frq**	**Best Numbers**
9	3	**9**	3	**2**	2	**7**	3	Most Draws
2	2	**4**	2	**3**	2	**2**	2	Second Most
3	-	-		**6**	2	**2**	2	Ties included
				7	2			Ties included

"#" is the number drawn; shown in bold type.
"Freq" is the frequency of occurrence shown in normal (non-bold) type.
"Best Numbers" displays the balls most frequently drawn, in order.
"Position 1" indicates the first ball drawn, "Position 2" the second ball drawn, and so on.
The final column notes the order of appearance, that is, the most occurrences (best or hottest numbers), then the second, third and fourth most occurrences, in order.

The results are early and it is hard to draw too many conclusions from a small sample such as this. However, there are strategies (called **burst strategies**) that draw on small sample sizes as part of larger plays. Unless you are running specialized Level III plays, you generally want to draw on decent-sized regression levels. That is what we'll do now.

Following is a Best Number Analysis of a 100-game drawing.

BEST NUMBER ANALYSIS
Four-Ball Lottery / 100 Drawings

Position 1		Position 2		Position 3		Position 4		
#	Frq	#	Frq	#	Frq	#	Frq	Best Numbers
1	16	0	18	0	15	2	14	Most Draws
8	15	8	13	2	14	1	13	Second Most
3	14	2	12	7	13	4	13	Third Most

These are your hottest numbers, by position, over the 100-game drawing sample. Only the top three positions are shown.

Playing Best Numbers

We have performed a Best Number Analysis of 100 drawings and extracted the top performing numbers, as above. So what do you do with these numbers? That's easy. Let's look at a few possibilities, playing one ticket and playing multiple tickets.

Playing One Ticket

In the above four-ball game Best Number Analysis, you see that number 1 (16 times) was the most drawn number in the first column, 0 (18 times) was the most popular in the second column, 0 again (15 times) was the top performer in the third column, and 2 (14 times) was the top performer in the fourth column.

Your Best Number Analysis has identified 1-0-0-2 as the top performing combination over a 100-game regression level.

If you were playing just one ticket, the 1-0-0-2 would be your combination to play. Even though the 8 in the first column was tied for the second most frequently drawn digit of all numbers drawn, it is not one of your top four numbers because the four-ball game (and the three-ball game as well) is analyzed by position. To form a ticket in a four-ball lottery game, you must pick four numbers, and with a Best Number Analysis you pick the top performing number from each position to get that four-digit combination.

The top performing numbers from each of the lottery bins are automatically going to be the four best numbers to play—they have already proven themselves in the field of battle.

What if you want a more aggressive approach, and want to attack the lottery with a bank of tickets? Let's look at that now.

Playing Multiple Tickets

If you are playing more than one ticket, you need more than four numbers to play. So how do you go about getting more chosen numbers?

The process is easy because you have already done your homework. Your positional analysis has identified the top-performing numbers, so you just have to decide how many of those numbers—and what criteria—you will use. For example, do you want to use the best numbers in the first two spots on all three positions? Maybe you want to use only the very best numbers, regardless of position. That could mean that you take, for example, three numbers from Position 1, one from Position 2, and two from Positions 3 and 4.

You have many possibilities on how to play your selections. You also have the further question of how many tickets to play, that is, the amount of money you want to invest in the lottery game. The more numbers you play, the more tickets you'll need to fully cover every possibility, but you need to be fiscally responsible and keep your ticket purchases to a reasonable level, "reasonable" being an amount that does not put you under emotional or financial duress.

If you pulled the top two numbers from each column, these are the numbers you would consider:

1	2	3	4	Positions
1	0	0	2	
8	8	2	1	

In Position 4, the 4 could be considered as well, since it was tied in appearances with number 1.

To play every combination of your top two numbers in a three-ball game would require a purchase of eight tickets. In a four-ball game, it would take a purchase of 16 tickets. It would look like this:

1-0-0-2	1-0-0-1	1-0-2-2	1-0-2-1
1-8-0-2	1-8-0-1	1-8-2-2	1-8-2-1
8-8-2-1	8-8-2-2	8-8-0-2	8-8-0-1
8-0-0-2	8-0-0-1	8-0-2-2	8-0-2-1

Most players, understandably, do not want to commit that much to a lottery game, especially if they play frequently. That kind of fiscal outlay would cost you thousands of dollars each year! Let's say you wanted to play just three tickets. You might choose these numbers:

1-0-0-2 (your best ticket)
1-0-2-2 (three top performing numbers and a second-best)
8-0-0-2 (three top performing numbers and a second-best)

If you extended your play to five tickets, you would choose two of the 13 remaining possibilities, but not the 8-8-2-1 since the individual digits have had less success than the other combinations in the group. (It would ignore all the top performing numbers in each position). The 8-8-2-1 ticket, however, is not a bad choice either since the numbers chosen are still top-two performing numbers!

If you were an aggressive player pushing a pool greater than 16 tickets, you would dig deeper into your best number pool and extend your coverage to the third or even fourth spots according to the criteria we just used to play three tickets.

In three-ball lotteries, there are fewer possibilities if you want to cover all the numbers, but just the same, you would still have to restrict your numbers to the top performers in combinations that keep you within budget.

In the "Wheeling" chapter, we will talk more about distributing multiple chosen numbers over a group of tickets so that you can get your main numbers in play at a reasonable cost.

Playing best numbers (hot numbers) is a strong strategy. Some players, however, think that best numbers have been overplayed and are due to grow cold. These players, contrarian thinkers much like wrong bettors in craps, instead want to opt for numbers that have not hit for a while. In other words, they want to play "overdue" or "cold" numbers.

Let's turn our attention to the next core strategy.

CORE STRATEGY #2:
OVERDUE NUMBER ANALYSIS
(COLD NUMBERS)

A powerful and popular core strategy, the *Overdue Number Analysis*, takes the opposite approach of a Best Number Analysis, and draws information from a Positional Analysis Refined Chart as well. An **Overdue Number Analysis** organizes and identifies numbers that have been the *least frequently drawn* over a specified number of games, and displays them in order of least frequently drawn to most frequently drawn—exactly the opposite of the Best Number Analysis.

You rely on the same charts you used to identify the hot numbers except that, in this particular case, you are going to extract the cold numbers.

An Overdue Number Analysis is counterintuitive to players who subscribe to the theory that you should play the numbers that get drawn more frequently than others. Some players like to go against the grain (and trends) for their profits, like wrong bettors (don't pass and don't come) in craps, and underdog bettors in sports. Some of these players have enjoyed great success going against the flow.

The theory is that, according to the law of averages, the hot numbers will regress back to the mean and the overdue numbers, which are underdrawn, will make up for lost ground by escalating in number of appearances.

Here is a copy of the Positional Drawing History chart used in the earlier 10-game drawing.

POSITIONAL DRAWING HISTORY
Four-Ball Lottery / 10 Games

	Position			
Date	**1**	**2**	**3**	**4**
9/1	9	4	4	1
9/2	2	0	2	7
9/3	9	7	5	7
9/4	6	4	7	0
9/5	5	9	3	3
9/6	8	3	7	7
9/7	4	9	6	2
9/8	2	2	3	8
9/9	9	8	6	9
9/10	1	9	2	2

Each horizontal row represents a four-ball drawing on the date indicated, and the columns chart the ball drawn in each of the four positions. Position 1 shows the first ball drawn, Position 2 shows the second ball drawn, Position 3 shows the third ball drawn, and Position 4 shows the fourth and last ball drawn.

You rearrange the numbers so that they are in order from fewest times drawn to most times drawn.

The Overdue Number Analysis on the following page shows what the chart looks like.

OVERDUE NUMBER ANALYSIS
4-Ball Lottery / 10 Drawings

Position 1		Position 2		Position 3		Position 4		
#	Frq	#	Frq	#	Frq	#	Frq	Overdue #s
0	0	**1**	0	**0**	0	**4**	0	Fewest Draws
3	0	**5**	0	**1**	0	**5**	0	Second Fewest
7	0	**6**	0	**8**	0	**6**	0	Third Fewest
-	-	-		**9**	0	-	-	Fourth Fewest

"#" is the number drawn shown in bold type.

"Freq" is the frequency of occurrence shown in normal (non-bold) type.

"Overdue Numbers" displays the balls least frequently drawn, in order.

"Position 1" indicates the first ball drawn, "Position 2" the second ball drawn, and so on.

The final column notes the order of appearance, that is, the fewest occurrences (overdue or cold numbers), then the second, third and fourth least occurrences, in order.

In the overdue numbers section, you see that Positions 1, 2 and 4 have three numbers that haven't been drawn a single time, and Position 3 has four numbers that haven't been drawn.

This sample size is so small that you have a lot of numbers that haven't yet had much of a chance to get drawn, showing that a 10-game Overdue Number Analysis in lottery is not sufficiently large enough to get significant results for playing cold numbers. In this 10-game analysis, there are 14 total numbers that haven't been drawn on a single occasion across the four positions.

You need a broader history to get a higher confidence level for choosing overdue numbers and forming tickets. Unless you are running a specialized short-term regression play as part of an advanced Level III strategy, I would recommend a regression level of at least 25 games.

Following is an Overdue Number Analysis for a 100-game drawing. We'll use the earlier results from the Positional Analysis Refined Chart though, of course, the results are flipped from a Best Number Analysis.

Here is the ame Positional Analysis Refined Chart that we extracted the data from.

POSITIONAL ANALYSIS REFINED CHART
4-Ball Lottery / 100 Drawings

	1	2	3	4
0	9	18	15	7
1	16	9	7	13
2	5	12	14	14
3	14	7	11	6
4	8	11	4	13
5	4	7	9	10
6	8	8	6	11
7	10	10	13	7
8	15	13	11	11
9	11	5	10	8

Following is an Overdue Number Analysis from these results.

OVERDUE NUMBER ANALYSIS
4-Ball Lottery / 100 Drawings

Position 1		Position 2		Position 3		Position 4		
#	Frq	#	Frq	#	Frq	#	Frq	Overdue #s
5	4	9	5	4	4	3	6	Fewest Draws
2	5	5	7	6	6	7	7	Second Fewest
6	8	3	8	1	7	0	7	Third Fewest
4	8	-	-	-	-	-	-	Ties included

These are your most overdue numbers, by position, over the 100-game drawing sampled. In Position 1, the tie for the fourth-most overdue numbers is listed.

Playing Overdue Numbers
You'll use the same positional analysis of the last 100 drawings for the three-ball lottery game as the Best Number Analysis; however, you care about the cold numbers so, instead, you organize the data into an Overdue Number Analysis. You're only going to play the top performing numbers on your tickets.

So what do you do with these numbers? You handle them as before, just like the best numbers. Let's look at a few possibilities, playing one ticket and playing multiple tickets.

Playing One Ticket
If you pulled the top two overdue numbers from each column, these are the numbers you would consider:

1	2	3	4	Positions
5	9	4	3	
2	5	6	7	

If you're playing one ticket, you would choose the top number in each column and your ticket would be 5-9-4-3.

Playing Multiple Tickets

Your decision as to how many of the overdue numbers you want to play, that is, how many tickets you want to have in action, is a function of how much money you want to commit to a game. The more numbers and number combinations you play, the greater the cost to you for playing lottery.

As with a Best Number Analysis, you must be selective in how many numbers you play on your tickets. If your budget is, say $5, then you choose only $5 worth of the very top performing numbers—the most overdue ones showing on your Overdue Number Analysis. You limit your numbers played to the very top performing ones and run with those tickets.

Let's say your budget is $3 for a lottery game. If you think an overdue numbers play is the right way to go, here are the numbers you might consider for your three tickets:

5-9-4-3 (your best ticket)
2-9-4-3 (three top performing numbers and a second best)
5-9-6-3 (three top performing numbers and a second best)

If you increased your play to five tickets, you would add two of the remaining 13 combinations of the top two performing positions, since they are the most important overdue number combinations.

If you were an aggressive player running a pool deeper than 16 tickets, you would bring more overdue numbers into play, perhaps extending your coverage to the third or even fourth spots, if you needed to, according to the criteria we just used to play three tickets.

In any case, the same principles apply for Best Numbers, Overdue Numbers or, really, numbers derived from any analysis that identifies chosen numbers. You choose the top performing numbers and play them in your tickets.

Often, you will have more numbers than you would want to play, but as discussed earlier in the Best Number Analysis section, using well designed wheels (see the *Wheeling* chapter) will allow you to distribute multiple chosen numbers over a group of tickets so that the dual goals of getting all your top performing numbers in play and at a reasonable cost can be achieved.

FIVE & SIX BALL LOTTO

THE BASICS OF PLAY

The five-ball and six-ball lotto games generate a tremendous amount of excitement among players. The huge jackpots, sometimes exceeding $100 million, offer enough money to do everything a person dreamed of in his or her life. And then some.

When those jackpots start swelling north of eight figures, they generate even more excitement and many more players begin chasing the dream.

There are many variations of five- and six-ball lotto games, but they all work more or less the same way. They all have a single pool containing all the balls in play. There may be as few as 25 balls in the pool, as in West Virginia, or as many as 59 balls, as in New York's lotto game, with many variations in between. Unlike lottery games, where there are multiple pools of balls, lotto games have just one pool of balls from which all the winning balls will be drawn.

In the five-ball games, five balls will be drawn, and in the six-ball games, six balls will be drawn. Your challenge is to correctly pick the numbers that will be selected. In the five-ball games, you can only mark five numbers on an individual ticket and if you choose all of them correctly, you hit the jackpot. If you get three or four of those numbers right, you win a lesser amount. Each state has different payout arrangements for the amount to be won, though the jackpot amount is a direct function of how much money was bet into the game by all the players who took a chance with their cash.

The more people that play or, to be more precise, the more tickets that are purchased, the greater the jackpot. And if the jackpot isn't hit, all the money earmarked for the big prize rolls over to the next drawing and proceeds to grow even larger as more people purchase even more tickets.

While you can only choose five numbers on an individual ticket, you may purchase as many tickets as you like. Many players will play five or 10 tickets, some might play two or three tickets, and a few very aggressive players will buy a whole bank of tickets in their quest to correctly pick the winning combination. There are still others, perhaps even a majority of players, who play exactly one ticket, minimizing their investment in the big dream to just $1 per game.

The six-ball games work exactly like the five-ball games except that six balls will be drawn from the pool and your tickets will be marked with exactly six numbers. Again, like the five-ball games, you may play as many tickets as you like. If you hit all six numbers correctly, congratulations, you're rich!

The fewer the number of balls in the pool, the easier it is to hit a jackpot. That's the advantage of playing games with a smaller pool of balls. But the advantage of playing games with a larger pool of balls is bigger jackpots. Much bigger jackpots.

The typical six-ball lotto game costs $1 to play and might feature a total pool of 49 balls, numbered 1-49, from which six balls will be chosen. As I said earlier, a wide range of balls can be in the pool, depending upon which state is offering the game. The numbers on those six balls will be the winning combination. For example, if the numbers drawn are 11-2-41-18-35-17, the life of the player who picked those exact six numbers can change in a hurry—he's hit the jackpot!

Smaller cash prizes will be awarded to tickets that contain five of the six drawn numbers, and also to tickets with three and four winning numbers. Tickets with just one or two of the drawn numbers, or no drawn numbers, win nothing.

While the six-ball lotto games with 49 total balls in the pool—called the **6/49 game**—are very popular, you will also find games with balls drawn from a larger pool. For example, a **6/51 game** will have a pool of 51 numbers from which the six winning balls will be drawn, and there is even a **6/54 game**. There are also games with fewer total balls in the pool, such as 6/42, 6/46, 6/47 and the aforementioned 6/25. Each state follows its own regulations for offering lotto games and has its own offerings.

Most six-ball lotto games are held biweekly with drawings typically on Wednesday and Saturday nights. If there are multiple winners for the jackpot, that is, if two or more players correctly pick all six numbers, the jackpot is split among them. If there are no winners, the jackpot rolls over to the next drawing, greatly increasing the following week's pool and making the game that much more exciting. If enough weeks go by without a winner, the potential jackpot starts making national news and everybody wants to get in on the act.

The amount of money you can win is entirely dependent on the total prize pool for that week, that is, the total number of tickets sold. Lotto is a **pari-mutuel game**, meaning that the total amount bet less the money taken by the government for its fees and costs, is available for the prize pool. The greater the number of tickets sold, the greater the jackpot.

The **five-ball lotto games**, also known as **little lottos**, draw from smaller pools of numbers, such as 36 or 39, and pick only five balls. The game works the same as the six-ball version, except that it is easier to win, though by no means is it "easy"—*all* lotto jackpots are giant longshots—since all five balls must be hit. Little Lotto games are played more frequently, often six or seven days a week, than the six-ball game. Fewer tickets are sold for the more frequent five-ball games, so the prizes are for much smaller amounts.

In any case, if you do hit all five numbers, you won't be complaining too much. You'll be too busy trying to figure out what to do with your money!

STRATEGY OVERVIEW

The foundation of all your winning strategies in lotto games is the powerful *frequency analysis* tool. **Frequency analysis** is the science of charting and statistically analyzing the winning balls from a specified number of previous drawings. A frequency analysis is used to identify the trends, streaks, tendencies, best numbers, overdue balls, combinations and a host of other data that you will extract to form your winning strategies.

In addition to these core strategies, you rely on frequency analysis to identify the various keys used in Level II strategies—such as kings, queens and exotic numbers—if you decide to continue your studies into advanced play. (See the back pages for information on advanced Level III strategies.)

In running a frequency analysis, you can choose as many games from a regression history as called for in the strategy you are using. I'll show you how to make these charts by hand so that you can use them to their full powers when employing exotic and advanced strategies. Online strategy programs such as *LotterySuperSystem.com* have many advantages over traditional hand-created databases, but the most compelling one is the ability to populate, store and analyze huge databases of previous winning balls and to get results with just the click of a few buttons.

To start the process of identifying the top performing balls for whatever analysis you will choose, you'll need to create a *Raw Frequency Analysis* chart. A **Raw Frequency Analysis Chart** displays this information in chart form. You extract data from the frequency analysis to identify numbers that you will use in your tickets under the theory that there is a bias in how prior numbers were drawn or a tendency of certain numbers to appear more often than others, either in the long run or short term.

Most strategies for lotto games in both the powerful Level 1 core strategies we cover here (and the advanced Level II and Level III strategies) rely on the results of frequency analysis.

HOW TO MAKE FREQUENCY ANALYSIS CHARTS

To create a Raw Frequency Analysis Chart, you start with a blank chart created specifically for this purpose. In the left column, you list the total number of balls in the game. In the second column, you record the balls as they appear, using dots or vertical lines (or whatever notation you're comfortable with) to indicate a drawn ball.

We are going to analyze a six-ball lotto game from the state of West Virginia. It is a 6/25 game, which, for purposes of illustration, allows us to get the full set of 25 numbers on a single page in this book.

FREQUENCY ANALYSIS
Blank Worksheet

1	
2	
3	
4	
5	
6	
7	
8	
9	
10	
11	
12	
13	
14	
15	
16	
17	
18	
19	
20	
21	
22	
23	
24	
25	

The first drawing, held on August 25, 2015, drew these six numbers: 1, 4, 19, 23, 24, 25.

You fill these numbers into your worksheet.

You do not break down balls by position, as in the Positional Charts for lottery games, because there is only one pool and all balls come from that same pool. (Remember that lottery has multiple pools and we keep track of each one separately.)

You only care about the total frequency of the numbers drawn and treat all numbers equally in this one chart. In a more advanced analysis, you would record the numbers in groups of 10 or 25 drawings so that you can keep both shorter-term and longer-term histories at the same time. But for now, you are only concerned with the simple but powerful core strategies.

The following page shows the chart after this first draw. Next will be a Raw Frequency Analysis worksheet with three games charted, then 25 games, in order. You'll see how the chart builds as more data from drawings gets added.

RAW FREQUENCY ANALYSIS CHART
Dot Results / 1 Lotto Game

1	•
2	
3	
4	•
5	
6	
7	
8	
9	
10	
11	
12	
13	
14	
15	
16	
17	
18	
19	•
20	
21	
22	
23	•
24	•
25	•

RAW FREQUENCY ANALYSIS CHART
Dot Results / 3 Lotto Games

1	••
2	
3	
4	••
5	•
6	
7	
8	•
9	•
10	
11	
12	•
13	
14	
15	
16	
17	
18	
19	••
20	•
21	•
22	
23	••
24	••
25	••

RAW FREQUENCY ANALYSIS CHART
Dot Results / 25 Lotto Games

1	••••••••
2	••••
3	••••••
4	•••••••••
5	•••••
6	••••••
7	•••
8	•••
9	•••••••••••
10	•••••••
11	••••••
12	•••••••
13	•••••
14	••••••
15	••••••
16	••
17	••••••
18	••••••
19	•••••••
20	•••••
21	•••••••
22	•
23	•••••••
24	•••••••••
25	•••••••••

Okay, you're looking at a bunch of dots. As with the lottery strategies, you want to convert that data into numbers. It is much easier to analyze the lottery when the data is listed in number form. To achieve this, you create a *Refined Frequency Analysis Chart*. In a **Refined Frequency Analysis Chart** all the dots from the Raw Frequency Analysis worksheets get converted into numbers.

This Raw Frequency Analysis chart on the previous page has the data from a 25-game regression level. You can do regression levels for any number of games—50 games, 75 games, 100 games, 150 games, 200 games, 250 games, whatever your strategy calls for. The next charts show a Refined Frequency Analysis for both a 25-game regression level and a 100-game regression level so that you can see how the data has developed.

These charts were extracted from actual drawings in the West Virginia Cash25 game. The 25-game regression level charted drawings between August 28, 2015 and October 9, 2015, and the 100-game regression level was from August 28 until February 18, 2016.

These two charts give you all sorts of data to work with. It just depends on your needs as to whether you'll draw results from the 25-game history or the 100-game history—or in the case of some Level III strategies, both of these regression levels (and many others as well).

You can either create separate charts, or just put a total column in your charts as I did here to keep the totals of each ball drawn.

REFINED FREQUENCY ANALYSIS CHART
25 Games / 6/25 Lotto Game

		Total
1	••••••••	8
2	••••	4
3	••••••	6
4	•••••••••	9
5	•••••	5
6	••••••	6
7	•••	3
8	•••	3
9	••••••••••	10
10	•••••••	7
11	••••••	6
12	•••••••	7
13	•••••	5
14	••••••	6
15	••••••	6
16	••	2
17	••••••	6
18	••••••	6
19	•••••••	7
20	•••••	5
21	•••••••	7
22	•	1
23	•••••••	7
24	•••••••••	9
25	•••••••••	9

REFINED FREQUENCY ANALYSIS CHART
100 Games / 6/25 Lotto Game

	Total
1	32
2	16
3	19
4	24
5	24
6	27
7	14
8	20
9	25
10	27
11	22
12	26
13	22
14	27
15	24
16	16
17	23
18	26
19	24
20	24
21	28
22	20
23	20
24	33
25	37

Now it's time to sort the information so that you can use core strategies and build tickets. You could base your tickets on the 25-game regression level or the 100-game level or, if you want, do a deeper search and build your tickets from the data drawn in a 150-game or even 250-game analysis. Choosing a regression level is a matter of strategic philosophy, or when you are using advanced Level II or Level III strategies, the particular strategy will dictate how deep (or shallow) a regression level you'll use.

The Refined Frequency Analysis (similar to the Positional Analysis for lottery) charts raw data that needs to be converted and refined into more usable charts, such as Best Number and Overdue Number Analyses.

LOTTO CORE ANALYSES

Let's look at the core analyses and see how you use them in lotto games. We'll start with the Best Number Analysis.

Best Number Analysis: Lotto

A Best Number Frequency Analysis takes the data from the Refined Frequency Analysis Chart and sorts it from numbers most frequently drawn to least frequently drawn. You're only going to be playing the very best numbers. Exactly how many is a function of the number of tickets you want to play or, to put it another way, the amount of money you want to invest in a game.

Following is a 100-game Best Number Analysis of the West Virginia Cash25 drawn between August 28, 2015 and February 18, 2016. The numbers of the Refined Frequency Analysis are sorted by most frequently drawn at the top, down to the least frequently drawn at the bottom.

BEST NUMBER ANALYSIS
100 Games / 6/25 Lotto Game

Best Number	Frequency	Rank
25	37	1
24	33	2
1	32	3
21	28	4
6	27	5
10	27	6
14	27	7
12	26	8
18	26	9
9	25	10
4	24	11
5	24	12
15	24	13
19	24	14
20	24	15
17	23	16
11	22	17
13	22	18
8	20	19
22	20	20
23	20	21
3	19	22
2	16	23
16	16	24
7	14	25

Overdue Number Analysis: Lotto

An **Overdue Frequency Analysis** sorts the data from a Raw Frequency Analysis Chart by order of least frequently drawn over a specified period of time to the most frequently drawn—the opposite of a Best Number Frequency Analysis. The number with the fewest total of occurrences is listed first, the second fewest total of occurrences second, and so on down to the numbers ranked by fewest occurrences.

The Overdue Frequency Analysis chart also shows the number of times the top performing overdue numbers have been drawn. While you only care about the 10 most overdue numbers, or perhaps the 12 or so most overdue—depending on your level of aggressiveness—you want to expand your working chart to include the top 20 or so, because overdue numbers are very fluid. As one drawing goes to the next, your overdue numbers might start getting hit (which is why you are playing them!) and other numbers outside your top chosen numbers may rise to the top.

If you're closely tracking only the top 10 overdue numbers, important overdue numbers that start rising in importance may get overlooked.

Following is an Overdue Number Analysis of the 100-game West Virginia Cash25 from earlier.

OVERDUE FREQUENCY ANALYSIS
100 Games / 6/25 Lotto Game

Best Number	Frequency	Rank
7	14	1
2	16	2
16	16	3
3	19	4
8	20	5
22	20	6
23	20	7
11	22	8
13	22	9
17	23	10
4	24	11
5	24	12
15	24	13
19	24	14
20	24	15
9	25	16
12	26	17
18	26	18
6	27	19
10	27	20
14	27	21
21	28	22
1	32	23
24	33	24
25	37	25

Your overdue charts will change rapidly as cold numbers get drawn and are no longer overdue, so you must keep on top of your numbers, game by game. For example, if the previously cold number 16 was drawn, you might have to move it down your most overdue list. If it was drawn a second time in succession, and then a third time, you would certainly be moving it down your overdue numbers list, and probably would move it right onto your best number list!

Every 10 or 20 games, you'll need to run a new Overdue Number Analysis to stay on top of the trends.

As you have seen, Overdue Number Charts track the frequency of numbers being drawn over a specified number of games. But there is another way to chart overdue numbers—by *length of time* since numbers have been drawn. I have developed specialized strategies to mine these excellent opportunities. These are called *Distance Charts*. You can find out more information about these Level III plays in the back pages of this book.

Playing Best Number and Overdue Number Tickets

Regardless of the strategy you'll be playing—best numbers, overdue numbers, clusters, lucky numbers (these latter two strategies will be covered later), whatever—you're going to concentrate your tickets on the top performing numbers extracted by your analysis. Once you've chosen your strategy, your first decision is to determine the regression level you'll be using. And then you have to decide the number of tickets you'll want to play.

You might analyze a regression depth of 25 games, 100 games, 150 games, 250 games, or some other depth that you think works best for the jackpots you'll be attacking. In the following example, you'll use the data from the 100-game regression level of the West Virginia Cash25 game presented earlier. Here are the top 10 results from that 100-game Best Number analysis:

BEST NUMBER FREQUENCY ANALYSIS
100 Games / Top 10 Results

Best Number	Frequency	Rank
25	37	1
24	33	2
1	32	3
21	28	4
6	27	5
10	27	6
14	27	7
12	26	8
18	26	9
9	25	10

Playing One Ticket

If you're going to buy just one ticket in the 6/49 game, you simply take the top six numbers and make that your ticket. Here is what that ticket would look like:

25-24-1-21-6-10

Here is the same group of numbers sorted from low number to high number:

1-6-10-21-24-25

Playing Multiple Tickets

Let's say you want to be more aggressive and play eight tickets, that is, invest $8 into the lotto game.

You like the top 10 numbers only, so that means you'll be working with 10 chosen numbers. In addition to a 10/8 play— 10 chosen numbers, 8 tickets—there is virtually an endless number of chosen-number/tickets-played combinations you could use, such as 10/10. 9/3, 9/5, 12/8. 12/15, 18/10, 11/18 and 8/3.

We looked at chosen numbers extracted from a Best Number Analysis in the example above, but the same principles apply for overdue numbers, lucky numbers (the subject of a separate chapter), or any other type of analysis that yields chosen numbers. You use your top performing numbers as part of the tickets you'll play. For example, if you wanted to play an 11/5 combination, you would choose the top 11 overdue numbers and spread them out on five tickets.

In the "Wheeling Strategies" chapter, we'll go over exactly how to efficiently combine numbers into tickets.

Let's look at one more core approach, Cluster Analysis, which you can use as part of your winning strategies.

CLUSTER ANALYSIS

Cluster analysis is the science of charting and statistically identifying and analyzing balls that have been drawn together in a specified number of individual lotto drawings. Numbers drawn together in an individual lotto drawing are called **clusters** or **paired numbers**. (You don't use a cluster analysis in lottery games because the balls are drawn from different chutes, not from the same pool of balls as in lotto games.)

Organizing Clusters

You want to identify all the clusters (paired groups) from a drawing. Let's say you're following a six-ball lotto game and the following numbers have been drawn:

In Order of Draw	Sorted
9 17 3 43 11 47	3 9 11 17 43 47

You display the paired groups in ascending order showing every possible combination because it is easier to identify the clusters with this kind of organization. It doesn't matter in which order the balls are drawn, only that they were drawn.

You always display paired groups by the smaller number first. Here are the paired groups:

CLUSTER COMBINATION CHART

Paired Groups (Clusters)					Groupings
3-9	3-11	3-17	3-43	3-47	("3" grouping)
9-11	9-17	9-43	9-47		("9" grouping)
11-17	11-43	11-47			("11" grouping)
17-43	17-47				("17" grouping)
43-47					("43" grouping)

Grouping classifies the paired numbers in a drawing by referencing the **anchor ball**, the lowest numbered ball in a cluster. You identify a cluster group first by naming its anchor ball. The first grouping, the "3" grouping, indicates that the 3 is the anchor ball. The highest numbered ball in a cluster is called the **chain ball**.

As you can see, the anchor ball of 3—that is, in the 3 grouping—has chain balls of 9, 11, 17, 43 and 47.

Technically, it doesn't matter whether a cluster is displayed as 3-9 or 9-3, or 43-47 or 47-43. In any of these cases, the two balls are drawn together so they are clusters. However, to keep your clusters organized and easy to match, you display them in ascending order.

To organize clusters, start with the lowest number and add combinations of every other drawn number. Then take the second lowest number and do the same, omitting any duplicates. Then the third number, fourth number and fifth number. You don't do this with the sixth number because it will be identical to the first, which you have already recorded. The lowest number will have five unique combinations; the second lowest will have four combinations; the third lowest, three combinations; the fourth lowest, two combinations; and the fifth lowest, one combination—just like you see in the Cluster Combination Chart.

There are 15 total unique clusters in this six-ball drawing. In all six-ball drawings, there will be exactly 15 unique clusters. In a five-ball drawing, there will be exactly 10 unique clusters.

Here is a breakdown on cluster groups in a six-ball lotto game, and then a five-ball lotto game:

CLUSTER GROUPINGS SIX-BALL LOTTO	
Anchor Ball	**Groupings**
Lowest	5
2nd Lowest	4
3rd Lowest	3
4th Lowest	2
5th Lowest	1
Total	15

CLUSTER GROUPINGS
FIVE-BALL LOTTO

Anchor Ball	Groupings
Lowest	4
2nd Lowest	3
3rd Lowest	2
4th Lowest	1
Total	10

Game	Cluster Groupings
5-Ball Game	10
6-Ball Game	15

FIVE-BALL DRAW EXAMPLE

In Order of Draw	Sorted
27 1 15 13 30	1 13 15 27 30

CLUSTER COMBINATION CHART

Paired Groups (Clusters)				Groupings
1-13	1-15	1-27	1-30	("1" Grouping)
13-15	13-27	13-30		("13" Grouping)
15-27	15-30			("15" Grouping)
27-30				("36" Grouping)

Repeating Clusters

A cluster analysis tries to identify **repeating clusters**; that is, clusters that repeat in two or more drawings. For example, the cluster pairs 11 and 14 might appear in two different drawings. That is a repeating cluster, the most powerful cluster formation. There are other types of cluster formations, but the repeating clusters are the ones you seek to find.

Let's look at three drawing groups and identify the clusters. The numbers have been sorted in ascending order.

A DRAWING	B DRAWING	C DRAWING
14 17 19 26 45 47	2 14 19 26 28 40	2 8 12 26 31 40

REPEATING CLUSTERS

	A & B DRAWING Repeating Clusters		B & C DRAWING Repeating Clusters
A	**14** 17 **19** 26 45 47	B	**2** 14 19 26 28 **40**
B	2 **14 19** 26 28 40	C	**2** 8 12 26 31 **40**

In the A and B drawings, 14 and 19 were repeating clusters, and in the B and C drawing, 2 and 40 were repeating clusters. In the chart, the repeating clusters are shown in underlined and bold type. These are just three sample drawings, hardly much of a sample, but they serve the purpose of showing you how to recognize repeating clusters.

As you add more drawings, the process of identifying repeating clusters becomes unwieldy, since there are 15 clusters in each draw. This is why you prefer computer software specifically set up to identify clusters such as *LotterySuperSystem.com* as opposed to identifying clusters by hand.

You can still identify repeating clusters by hand—but it's just a lot of work!

To be useful, a cluster analysis requires a much larger sample of games than just three games because repeating clusters don't come up that frequently. But if you track a sufficient number of games, you'll identify repeating clusters. These are very powerful numbers to play in your tickets.

7

POWERBALL & MEGA MILLIONS

The huge multi-state games such as Powerball and Mega Millions are so widely played that they deserve their own chapter. After all, with jackpots that dangle tens of millions of dollars as a throwaway hors d'oeuvre and over one-half billion dollars as a king's feast, it is hard not to get excited. Pretty much anything money can buy can be achieved if you take down one of these jackpots.

Mega-Millions and Powerball, the two largest multi-state lottery games, are played in more than 40 states and get the most attention because they accumulate the largest jackpots. The increase in price of the Powerball ticket to $2 and the lengthening in odds for Mega Millions in the early 2010s have accounted for the huge increase in jackpots compared to prior years. Both Mega Millions and Powerball have had multiple jackpots in excess of *one-half billion dollars*—an insane amount of money—and tons more in the hundreds of millions of dollars. The granddaddy of them all occurred in early 2016 when three lucky winners hit a $1.6 *billion* jackpot. Wow!

These two big **multi-state games** feature balls drawn from two separate drums, one with five balls, the other with just one ball. To win the jackpot, you must correctly pick all six balls.

Powerball drawings are held every Wednesday and Saturday night at 10:59 pm Eastern Standard Time. Five balls are drawn out of a drum with 69 white balls and one ball is drawn out of a drum with 26 red balls. The winner or winners of the jackpot (won by correctly picking the five white balls and the one red

Powerball) can choose to get 30 payouts over 29 years (the first payment occurs immediately) or a one-time payment of the entire jackpot. The second prize (won by correctly picking the five white balls) is $1,000,000 and is paid out in one lump sum. It costs $2 to play Powerball.

Mega Millions drawings are held every Tuesday and Friday at 11:00 pm Eastern Standard Time. Like Powerball, there are two pools of balls. One pool contains 75 white balls, out of which five balls are drawn, and a second pool contains 15 gold balls, from which one ball is drawn. The jackpot starts at $15 million and grows by a minimum of $5 million each time it is not hit. Winners can take the jackpot in one lump sum (equal to all the cash in the Mega Millions jackpot pool) or take the money in 30 payments, one upon winning, and one each over the next 29 years. The second prize, as in Powerball, is $1,000,000. It costs $1 to play Mega Millions.

Multi-state games are offered in all U.S. states that offer lotto and lottery games; however, some are regional in nature, such as Tri-State Megabucks Plus, which is played only in Vermont, New Hampshire and Maine. There are other popular multi-state games, including Hot Lotto, Lucky for Life, Wild Card 2, 2by2, and MegaHits.

Six states ban lottery-type games: Nevada, Utah, Mississippi, Alabama, Alaska and Hawaii.

DUAL-POOL STRATEGY 1

In dual–pool games like Mega Millions and Powerball, you have two pools to analyze—the five-ball pool and the one-ball pool—so it is more work, but of course, you have a greater reward at the end of the tunnel. Prizes are massive, way beyond life changing, but with so many balls in play, the odds of winning are astronomical. To give yourself a better chance, you want to be more aggressive with your tickets, but not at the expense of hurting yourself financially. Money management must always be at the heart of any winning strategy.

We'll save the money management discussion for that very important chapter. For now, let me just say that you have to consider what you are willing to risk without putting yourself in any kind of uncomfortable situation, either financially or emotionally.

I have given you all the tools to analyze these games, which you handle just like the other lotto and lottery games. You gather the data and run the appropriate core analyses that you will be using to attack the jackpot, whether it is a Best Number Analysis, an Overdue Number Analysis or a Cluster Analysis, along with any Lucky Numbers you want to play.

DUAL-POOL STRATEGY 2

In *Lottery Super System*, I go into a much deeper analysis of the games, but for here, let's just get right to the heart of the matter. There is a lot of money involved, plenty to go around if you're lucky enough to get a piece of a huge jackpot. Your best bet to shor10 the odds by many multiples is to run a *Big Wheel* strategy.

A **Big Wheel** strategy is a pool of multiple players who act together as a syndicate to buy a block of tickets and share winning prizes. Rather than having a relatively small bank of tickets playing on your own, you increase your net of plays—and your odds of winning—by tenfold, even one hundredfold when you form a syndicate of like-minded players!

8

USING LUCKY NUMBERS

Okay, I understand. You have lucky numbers you just have to play. That's fine. I'm not going to stop the tide from coming in or going back out again. I'll work with it instead.

The key to working with your lucky numbers is to incorporate them into your winning strategies. So, if you have identified eight chosen numbers through one of the other core analysis methods we discussed here, you can add another number or two to your pool of numbers. This gives you the best of both worlds.

TWO ADVANTAGES OF USING LUCKY NUMBERS

1. You have a solid pool of the top performing numbers to play, ones you have identified through your core analyses and you add your must-play lucky numbers, giving your tickets the added zest they might otherwise be lacking. If the numbers are indeed lucky, you *do* want them as part of your tickets.

2. You have a wider net of important numbers to try to catch a winning ticket. By dint of playing more numbers, you have a greater chance of catching a jackpot.

Let's run through an example of how you would play your lucky numbers. Through one of your core analyses, you have identified nine numbers as your top performers. These numbers are as follows: 8-11-12-14-24-28-31-41-45. You want to add two lucky numbers, 22 and 44, to your pool of chosen numbers.

So now your pool of 11 chosen numbers looks like this:

8-11-12-14-**22**-24-28-31-41-**44**-45

Your two lucky numbers appear in **bold**. Of course, you can make a ticket with all lucky numbers, but what kind of strategy would that be?

You could also have a pool of lucky numbers that you like and only play them when they match criteria from another analysis—in which case you play those numbers with a greater confidence, that is, on more tickets than other tickets. (This is called a **Lucky Number Key**. How to work lucky numbers in tickets is discussed in my book, *Lottery Super System*, and also in several of the Level III Advanced Strategies.)

You want to restrict lucky number play to a maximum of three chosen numbers. If you feel you must have more chosen numbers in your tickets, I suggest you play an additional ticket or two solely with lucky numbers so as not to dilute the main tickets you create with the analyses you learned in this book.

We discussed identifying chosen numbers from core analyses in the previous chapter, and using and adding lucky numbers to the pool in this one. Now let's see how to put these together into tickets you'll actually play.

It's time to talk about wheeling.

9

WHEELING STRATEGIES

If you were to play every one of your chosen numbers in every possible combination, it would cost you a fortune. For example, let's say your analyses produced a pool of 10 chosen numbers and you wanted them covered in every possible combination in a six-ball game. It would cost you $462!

That is not very practical, nor is it very sensible. But there is a way to get all your chosen numbers covered at a reasonable cost. The idea is to get good coverage of your chosen numbers in a system so that if they get drawn, you have an excellent chance of winning prizes without spending a ridiculous amount of money.

That is where *wheeling systems*, or *wheels*, come into play.

THE VALUE OF WHEELS

A **lottery wheel**, or simply a **wheel** or **wheeling system**, is a system of strategically distributing chosen numbers that gives a player partial coverage of all possible combinations such that a group of tickets can be played at a reasonable cost. Technically, I am referring to an **abbreviated wheeling system**, but for ease of discussion, I will stick with the simple term "wheel" to indicate strategically constructed combinations of numbers and use the term **full wheel** to describe the type of wheel where every single combination is covered.

Wheels provide a wide coverage of your chosen numbers without your having to play every combination. Obviously, the more combinations you cover, the greater the expense to play your numbers; however, you don't want to break the bank if you have, say, 11 or 12 numbers. The idea of the wheeling systems is to reduce that risk while still giving you an efficient coverage of your chosen numbers.

With luck you may win several prizes from your set of numbers. If you're very lucky, you may win the big jackpot.

You can use as many numbers in your wheels as you want; however, an individual number is used only one time per wheeling system. For example, if you've chosen these nine numbers—1-4-5-12-19-21-23-33, 45—you would choose a wheeling system to distribute them to the number of tickets you elect to play.

THE COST OF PLAYING EVERY CHOSEN NUMBER

You must select a minimum of six numbers in a six-ball game (or five numbers in a five-ball game) to be able to play a ticket. When you select exactly six numbers to work with, your bets are easy. There is only one possible combination of those six numbers. You would be playing a full wheel. Remember, in lotto as opposed to lottery games, it makes no difference in what order the numbers get chosen. If the six numbers you picked are drawn, you're a winner. For example, if you chose 8-13-15-24-42 and the drawing numbers came in this order, 24-8-42-15-13, you have won.

The complications for playing your numbers occur when you want to play a wider spread of numbers than the minimum six-number ticket so that every possible combination is covered. For example, if you choose 10 numbers to play, it would cost you $210 to play every combination possible for a full wheel—$1 for each every ticket to cover all 210 combinations. That's way too much money to invest in a lotto game.

If you wanted to play those 10 numbers per game, two times per week, you'd have to invest over $20,000 in a single year. That's a lot of money—a ridiculous amount of money—to spend on lotto tickets.

What if you add another number or play one fewer number and want to play all combinations? The following chart shows you how many six-ball tickets you would need to cover every chosen number in your pool and have a full wheel.

COMBINATIONS NEEDED FOR A FULL WHEEL

Numbers Chosen	All Combinations
6	6
7	7
8	28
9	84
10	210
11	462
12	924
13	1,716
14	3,003
15	5,005
16	8,008
17	12,376
18	18,564
19	27,132
20	38,760
21	54,264
22	74,613
23	100,947
24	134,596
25	177,100

Since each ticket costs $1 to play, you can see how crazy playing a full wheel can be. If you were an aggressive player covering 13 numbers, you would be looking at a cost of $5,005 to play a full wheel of every combination. That would be for just one drawing!

That's where wheeling systems come into play. By using a wheel, you are able to cover a large group of numbers without burying yourself under a pile of lotto tickets. The secret, as many serious lotto and lottery players have learned, is to combine your numbers into groups of tickets such that all your numbers are in play—but at a fraction of the cost.

You start the process by creating a *letter conversion chart*. Let's look at that now.

LETTER CONVERSION CHART

A **letter conversion chart** assigns one letter to each chosen number so that your chosen numbers can be inserted into a wheel template. For example, if you were using 10 chosen numbers in a wheel, you would use the first 10 letters of the alphabet, thus: A, B, C, D, E, F, G, H, I and J. If you were using eleven numbers, you would add the letter K, and if you used only seven chosen numbers, you would need only the letters A though G.

Let's say you ran an analysis and came up with seven chosen numbers—9, 17, 20, 21, 27, 31, 40. You set up a letter conversion chart, as follows.

LETTER CONVERSION CHART

<u>A</u>	<u>B</u>	<u>C</u>	<u>D</u>	<u>E</u>	<u>F</u>	<u>G</u>
9	17	20	21	27	31	40

Each letter represents a position on the wheel and the numbers below the letter represents your chosen numbers. You could match any letter with any number. For example, your conversion chart could look like this:

LETTER CONVERSION CHARTS

A	B	C	D	E	F	G
40	31	27	21	20	17	9

Or it could look like this:

A	B	C	D	E	F	G
9	27	31	21	40	17	20

We're using the Letter Conversion Chart as a device to disperse your chosen numbers into preset wheels to form tickets. The actual wheel is a matrix with the letters in position ready to be replaced by numbers. For ease of organization, it's generally best to list your numbers in ascending order, as we originally did. Here is our original Letter Conversion Chart.

LETTER CONVERSION CHART

A	B	C	D	E	F	G
9	17	20	21	27	31	40

WHEEL TEMPLATE

To organize your chosen numbers so that you can play them in powerful combinations, you use a simple *wheel template*. A **wheel template** matches letters of a wheeling system with chosen numbers so that you can create wheels with good coverage of the numbers you'll be playing.

Here is a wheel template for seven chosen numbers and seven games:

WHEEL TEMPLATE						
7 Chosen Numbers / 7 Tickets						
1.	A	B	C	D	E	F
2.	A	B	C	D	E	G
3.	A	B	C	D	F	G
4.	A	B	C	E	F	G
5.	A	B	D	E	F	G
6.	A	C	D	E	F	G
7.	B	C	D	E	F	G

You replace every letter symbol with the chosen number that corresponds to it from your Letter Conversion Chart. For example, the letter A gets replaced with 9, and the letter B with 17. The chart below has replaced all the letters with the corresponding numbers from the wheel template to show the final tickets you'll be playing.

LEVEL I WHEEL						
7 Chosen Numbers / 7 Tickets						
1.	9	17	20	21	27	31
2.	9	17	20	21	27	40
3.	9	17	20	21	31	40
4.	9	17	20	27	31	40
5.	9	17	21	27	31	40
6.	9	20	21	27	31	40
7.	17	20	21	27	31	40

In this particular wheel, each of your seven chosen numbers is played exactly six times across the seven tickets. At $1 a play, your cost for this set of seven tickets would be $7.

While this seven chosen number/seven ticket wheel has equal distribution of your chosen numbers, your wheels typically will have a slightly uneven distribution where one number, or a few numbers, might be played one more or one less time than the others simply because of the math.

This is perfectly fine. The goal in a Level I template is to keep your chosen numbers about evenly distributed across your tickets. Having a few numbers appear on one extra ticket, or one fewer ticket as the case may be, is just as good as equal distribution, for all intents and purposes. The point is, since your chosen numbers have equal importance, you want the distribution of them to be about equal as well. That is achieved in the wheel shown above, as well as in the following wheel.

Following is a 9-number, 8-ticket wheel template displaying about an equal distribution of your chosen numbers. All your chosen numbers are played five times on the eight tickets, except for the numbers represented by the A, B and C positions, which are played six times.

As before, you start the process of creating a set of wheeled tickets by creating a Letter Conversion Chart as a tool to easily organize and prepare your chosen numbers for insertion into a wheel template. Since you're working with nine numbers—2-6-15-20-26-32-35-37-41—you need nine letters, with each letter representing a chosen number. Hence, you use the letters A through I.

LETTER CONVERSION CHART

A	**B**	**C**	**D**	**E**	**F**	**G**	**H**	**I**
2	6	15	20	26	32	35	37	41

Now, here is a preset template designed for nine chosen numbers and eight tickets:

	WHEEL TEMPLATE					
	9 Chosen Numbers / 8 Tickets					
1.	A	B	C	E	F	H
2.	A	B	C	E	G	H
3.	A	B	D	E	G	H
4.	A	B	D	E	G	I
5.	A	C	D	F	G	I
6.	A	C	D	F	G	I
7.	B	C	D	F	H	I
8.	B	C	E	F	H	I

This is a strong wheel that gives about equal distribution to your important numbers, that is, your chosen numbers. You replace the template letters with your chosen numbers and come up with the following eight tickets, ready to go. Remember, the goal here is to get about equal distribution of your strong chosen numbers.

	LEVEL I WHEEL					
	9 Chosen Numbers / 8 Tickets					
1.	2	6	15	26	32	37
2.	2	6	15	26	35	37
3.	2	6	20	26	35	37
4.	2	6	20	26	35	41
5.	2	15	20	32	35	41
6.	2	15	20	32	35	41
7.	6	15	20	32	37	41
8.	6	15	26	32	37	41

The eight tickets are displayed with your chosen numbers, from left to right, as called for by the 9-chosen-number/8-ticket wheel. The first ticket is comprised of the numbers 2, 6, 15, 26, 32 and 37, the second ticket contains the numbers 2, 6, 15, 26, 35, and 37, and so on down to the eighth ticket, which uses the numbers 6, 15, 26, 32, 37 and 41.

All you need to do now is go to your lottery vendor, give him $8 and your set of eight tickets, and wait, hopefully, for some real good news when the numbers are drawn.

MORE ADVANCED STRATEGIES

I have shown you how to work with Level I wheels and systems, strategies that are powerful tools you can use to beat lotto and lottery games. And as you become more advanced in your approach to beating lottery games, you will sometimes use *uneven* distribution of your chosen numbers.

What's this about?

In Level II and Level III strategies, you isolate certain numbers among your chosen numbers as more important than the other numbers in your pool of chosen numbers and emphasize these more important numbers in your wheels. I call these numbers **keys**. Almost all advanced play centers around identifying these keys and playing them in strong combinations and wheels. But don't worry, the material I've covered in this book gives you powerful methods of attacking lotto and lottery jackpots. The Level II and Level III strategies rely on and build upon the Level I strategies.

You also want a full range of powerful Level I wheels in your arsenal to optimize various combinations of chosen numbers while maintaining the flexibility of buying few tickets or many tickets, depending upon the game and the circumstances.

Professional-level wheel packages are available for purchase at *www.cardozabooks.com* or from the ads in the back of this book, or you can go online to *www.lotterysupersystem.com*. The site will automatically create powerful wheels for you according to the parameters that you set.

Two More Wheels

Below are two more wheels you can use. Both feature equal distribution of your chosen numbers. The first wheel is set up for 10 chosen numbers and five tickets, and the second for 12 chosen numbers and six tickets. Before each wheel is a blank Letter Conversion chart. You would just fill in the chosen numbers under each letter.

In the back of this book you can find strategy packages containing a wealth of wheels designed specifically for the lotto.

LETTER CONVERSION CHART

A	B	C	D	E	F	G	H	I	J
x	x	x	x	x	x	x	x	x	x

WHEEL TEMPLATE
10 Chosen Numbers / 5 Tickets

1.	A	B	D	F	G	I
2.	A	C	D	F	H	I
3.	A	C	E	F	H	J
4.	B	C	E	G	H	J
5.	B	D	E	G	I	J

LETTER CONVERSION CHART

A	**B**	**C**	**D**	**E**	**F**	**G**	**H**	**I**	**J**	**K**	**L**
x	x	x	x	x	x	x	x	x	x	x	x

WHEEL TEMPLATE
12 Chosen Numbers /8 Tickets

1.	A	C	E	G	I	K
2.	A	C	E	G	I	K
3.	A	C	E	G	I	K
4.	A	C	E	G	I	K
5.	B	D	F	H	J	L
6.	B	D	F	H	J	L
7.	B	D	F	H	J	L
8.	B	D	F	H	J	L

⑩
THE WINNING APPROACH

The enormous number of lotto and lottery players who have defeatist attitudes amazes me! They lose game after game and grumble about their bad luck and the hopelessness of their tickets, yet they continue to play more tickets and make no effort to change their situation.

Does that kind of piss-poor attitude affect your winning chances at lotto and lottery games?

Absolutely.

It won't affect the *odds* of the games, but it will affect your chances of overcoming them. Because, whether you're the most optimistic person playing or the most negative, once the die is cast, so to speak, the odds are the odds. The lottery games won't care how you feel because they won't know. If you and I play 10 games each, it won't matter whether you or I mark the numbers or submit the tickets, or whether those perfunctory tasks will be performed by the most pessimistic person that can be found. The result will be the result, regardless of your mood or attitude, or what your horoscope might say.

The balls to be drawn have no idea about what you're thinking or feeling. I know that is a revolutionary statement for many players, but that is a mathematical truth.

These inanimate balls aren't receiving the mysterious human gamma ray messages telling them what to do. Not from me, not from you, not from the psychics or seers or fortunetellers, and not from each individual of the millions of players who think that the way they feel, good or bad, optimistic or pessimistic, positive or negative, will be uniquely responsible for the outcome of those headless and brainless plastic balls. Imagine that? Somehow the lotto and lottery balls are psychically bound to millions of players' beliefs and have only one outcome to fulfill all of those wishes. Now that's a tough ticket to deliver! It's mathematically impossible to perfectly satisfy two diverse tickets in one drawing, let alone millions.

Those small plastic spheres are simply balls after all, pieces of plastic with no more capacity to understand human emotions or be affected by them than a grain of sand on a beach.

But while attitude might not affect the chances of certain balls getting drawn, how you feel definitely affects your chances of winning. A player that plays with the goal of winning does everything he or she can do to achieve that goal. This player prepares properly—and preparation in life is everything for people on the track to succeed—and this player will make good money management decisions. This player will also make prudent decisions in all aspects of choosing numbers and buying tickets.

The loser, on the other hand, has losing writ10 all over him—in his actions, his moods, and of course, his results. No crowbar will pry him away from his bad plays until he's managed to lose his money. To be sure, the lotteries hold a huge edge, but players can still win. That is, the *smart* players can. Follow the advice in this book and you'll become a smart player, the one player who may buck the odds and surprise everyone.

11

THE REALITY & ODDS OF PLAYING LOTTERY GAMES

You play lotto and lottery games in the hope of making somewhere between a lot of money and an absolute fortune. You're chasing a dream that, if everything falls right, will change your life. That's all well and good, as long as you understand the realities, odds and risks involved in playing lottery games.

Let's not sugarcoat this. The odds against winning a big jackpot are astronomical, no matter what strategy you employ, and your chances of winning overall—between small wins, medium wins, and jackpots—are poor. Lotto and lottery are negative expectation games and the odds of coming out ahead are greatly against you. The state-run games, or any other entity running a lottery or lotto type game, have a huge mathematical edge over you and no amount of strategy and number prediction changes these expectations.

So why play the game?

You want to chase the big dream. I get it. When jackpots get huge, or even ridiculously huge as it did in January of 2016 when a Powerball prize reached $1.6 billion, you want to take a shot at it. It's hard not to get excited. A prize like that is more money than most people can even imagine.

But let me make this clear: If playing lottery games is your idea of making a living, it is a very bad idea. The odds are massively against you and you can count on lotto and lottery games costing you a lot of money in the long run—unless you are one of the few who can accumulate enough smaller wins to make a small profit or are one of the lucky few that hit the jackpot.

People do win, of course, and that's why others play. As the slogan of the New York lottery goes, "Hey, you never know."

If you follow the strategies in this book, your chances of winning will increase. Be warned, however, that they do not change the fundamental percentage disadvantage you face in the lottery games you play. But like I said earlier, the strategies in this book give you a fantastic approach for trying to beat lotto and lottery games.

First and foremost, as I will make clear in the money management chapter, let me emphasize this extremely important piece of advice: Never risk needed money at lotto and lottery, no matter how lucky you feel. The reality of playing lottery games is that money can be lost, and if that money is earmarked for rent or food, or any other necessity in your life, you're making a whopping mistake. I know this is all common sense, but it bears repeating because so many players go against this basic rule and put themselves in a bad situation.

Now that I've covered the basics, let's look at some of the odds of the game.

LOTTO ODDS

There is a big difference between the lotto games using 54 balls, such as Lotto Texas in Texas, and games using 25 balls, as in the West Virginia Cash 25 game. Quite simply, the more balls in play, the harder it is for you to win. Each ball that gets added to a pool of balls greatly increases the difficulty of choosing all five or six balls correctly, which is why lotto games with 54 balls take, on average, longer to hit a winning combination than a 49-ball pool, which in turn will get hit much less frequently than games with 39 balls, 36 balls, and 25 balls, respectively.

For example, in the 6/25 West Virginia lotto game (six balls get picked from a pool of 25 total balls), your chances of choosing all six numbers with one ticket are 1 in 177,100. In a 6/49 game, picking all six balls correctly has odds of 1 in 13,983,816. If the game is a 6/54, your chances of choosing all six numbers correctly out of the 54 balls in the pool with one ticket balloons to 1 in 25,827,165. That's just one chance in more than twenty-five million—astronomically difficult odds and a massive jump in difficulty.

Or, as I like to put it, you went from astronomical odds of hitting the jackpot to much more astronomical odds.

Here is a chart that shows the odds against hitting a jackpot in various games:

ODDS OF HITTING THE BIG JACKPOT	
Game	**Odds**
6/25	1 in 177,100
6/49	1 in 13, 983,816
6/54	1 in 25,827,165
Mega Millions	1 in 258,890,850
Powerball	1 in 292,201,338

You increase the odds of winning by playing better numbers and obtaining more tickets, but you are still up against a mountain of difficulty. I understand that you're not playing for the odds but for the chance of beating them, hoping that a few dollars invested will change everything in your life. Just don't lose sight of the chances against you hitting a jackpot. Let's look at the odds against winning some popular games.

Odds of Winning: 6/49 Game

The 6/49 game gives you the following chances of getting a winner with a single ticket:

6/49 LOTTO GAME ODDS

Balls Picked Correctly	Odds of Picking Winning Combination
6	1 in 13,983,816
5	1 in 54,201
4	1 in 1,032
3	1 in 57
Odds to win any prize	1 in 54

Odds of Powerball

POWERBALL ODDS

Match White Ball		Match Red Ball	Chances of Hitting*
5	and	1	1 in 292,201,338
5	and	0	1 in 11,688,054
4	and	1	1 in 913,129
4	and	0	1 in 36,525
3	and	1	1 in 14,494
3	and	0	1 in 579
2	and	1	1 in 701
1	and	1	1 in 92
0	and	1	1 in 38
Odds to win any prize			1 in 25

*Based on the standard $2 play. Numbers are rounded to nearest whole number.

Odds of Mega Millions

MEGA MILLIONS ODDS		
Match White Ball	Match Gold Ball	Chances of Hitting
5 and	1	1 in 258,890,850
5 and	0	1 in 18,492,204
4 and	1	1 in 739,688
4 and	0	1 in 52,835
3 and	1	1 in 10,720
3 and	0	1 in 766
2 and	1	1 in 473
1 and	1	1 in 56
0 and	1	1 in 21
Chance of hitting any prize		1 in 14.7

Long Odds Big Jackpot, Longer Odds Huge Jackpot

A $1 bet on a lotto ticket can win you millions, even hundreds of millions of dollars. Another way to view this is that it takes millions of losing $1 tickets by other players to build the jackpot for your win. You often have a choice of whether you'll go for a jackpot worth hundreds of thousands of dollars, millions of dollars, or hundreds of millions of dollars.

With all else equal, of course you'd go for the bigger jackpot. But all else is not equal.

The fewer the numbers in a lottery or lotto game pool, the greater your chances are of winning. As an extreme example, if there were only 12 numbers in the pool and picking the correct six numbers would make you a winner, your chances of winning would be very high—50%. Your payout in this particular game, if it were offered, would not be very much.

Conversely, the more numbers in the pool of numbers to be drawn, the more difficult it is to choose the winning combination, and concomitantly, the larger the winning jackpots tend to be.

There is a tradeoff between jackpots that are more difficult to win because of the greater pool of numbers and ones that are "easier" to win because of the smaller pool. Easier, in this sense, is a strange word to use because no jackpot in any lottery game is *easy* to win. You're always up against astronomical odds, even in the games with the smallest pools.

However, the games with the longest odds get the most fantastic of jackpots and those are the games that really make players excited. After all, why go for a million or two when you could go for a hundred million or several hundred million? Or, as occurred in mid-January 2016, when winners in three states—Florida, Tennessee, and California—shared a jackpot of $1.6 *billion*.

12
MONEY MANAGEMENT

The more tickets you play the greater your chances of winning prizes. That goes for all lotto and lottery games regardless of format, as well as bingo, church raffles, keno and any other type of game where a drawing is involved. There are many lotto and lottery games out there—three-ball, four-ball, five-ball, six-ball, Powerball and many other variations, you name it. And they all share the same principle: Play more tickets, increase your chances to win more prizes.

But that comes at a cost. More money. Everyone can figure that out. But what everyone does not figure out is exactly the cost of that cost. At least, not until it's too late. There are numerous stories of people who have slowly or rapidly invested their life savings in the games by following "the more, the better" theory.

You can make a lot of money playing lotto and lottery games—after all, that's why you chase jackpots every week and why you purchased this book—but at the same time, an aggressive player can get drained of needed resources if he or she consistently chases too hard week in and week out. As in all forms of gambling, it is important to view lottery games as a form of entertainment and to allocate a budget for that entertainment.

In other words, you must gamble within your means.

You have to decide how much money you have available as an entertainment budget. There is no guarantee of winning in any form of gambling, no matter how perfectly the stars may align, and that is certainly the case when playing the lottery.

You'll have small wins along the way and strings of weeks where you don't cash a single ticket. You can't ever expect to win money. That's just not practical. Overall, you're playing against big odds at the lottery and those odds are very hard to overcome. It is prudent to remind you that there are only a relatively few big jackpot winners, and you might not become one of those few. Meanwhile, week in and week out—if you are a weekly player—the lottery games will steadily ding your funds. You must be able to handle the losses.

Players are enticed by the big jackpots that can be won with the purchase of a single $1 ticket or a group of such tickets. Where else in life can you hope to get such massive payouts for such a small investment? When the jackpots get bigger and bigger and hit hundreds of millions of dollars, lottery fever goes wild and the net of players increases, making the jackpots even larger and the frenzy even greater.

And everyone is thinking, "That just might be me." You know something? Yes, it just might be. *You might be the next $100 million winner!*

Let's go back to that $1 ticket. It's not much of an investment for the hope of hitting a life-changing jackpot. But the reality is that it's not just $1. The investment may be for five tickets for $5, or 10 tickets for $10. There are players who play an even greater number of tickets, betting $20, $25, $50 and even hundreds of dollars. That's *just for one week*. And there are lots of weeks in a year. Fifty-two of them, to be precise. If you play the lotto weekly, or even daily, that money adds up fast. For too many players, the lottery becomes a serious financial investment with not enough return.

So it's not just $1.

If you spend $20 per week on various tickets, your lottery investment will be over $1,000 in a year. For people scraping to get by, that might not be money well spent. One thousand dollars is not a trivial amount. Bigger players invest much more than that in the lottery. Much, much more. Do the real math of how much you spend yearly on lotto and lottery games and the cold, hard numbers might be scary.

So how much should you invest in the pursuit of the dream jackpot? What does your strategy suggest for an investment?

Both questions have a real easy answer. It's the same type of answer that all gamblers face—poker players, blackjack players, slots players, bingo players, whoever—but the answer is different for different people. It is this: Spend whatever amount makes sense for you and your life. Whatever your situation, you must always follow this dictate.

Never gamble with money you cannot afford to lose, either financially or emotionally.

You need to be smart with your money. If $20 a week cuts into your needs, you shouldn't be buying $20 worth of lottery tickets and you certainly shouldn't be buying $30 or even $50 per week either. And if losing that $20 causes you to be emotionally upset, you have to ask yourself, "What am I doing?"

Be smart with your money, be smart with yourself. No gambling pursuit, no matter how favorable or attractive, guarantees that you will win. No matter how lucky you feel, it won't change the odds of a game and it won't change your chances of winning. You must be prepared to lose your investment, because it very well might happen. You should only play lotto and lottery games with discretionary income, money you don't mind losing and that won't hurt you financially or emotionally if you do lose.

Sure, it's nice to pursue the dream, but not at the expense of reality. If you heed common sense and play within your emotional and financial needs, you'll never get hurt at the game.

And you know what? You just may get lucky.

LUCK & SENSIBILITY

Determining the correct bankroll for you as a player is not just about the money you can afford to risk at lotto and lottery; it's also about what you can afford to lose emotionally. *There is no rule more important in all of gambling.*

The possibilities of taking a loss are real and if that loss will hurt, you're playing like a fool. It is inevitable that players who risk money over their means will lose more than they can afford. Luck won't help these players because even when the good music comes their way, as it surely will sometimes, they won't quit while they're ahead. They keep on going and going and going until the inevitable losses occur.

Gambling with needed funds is a foolish gamble. However, if you never play over your head, you'll never suffer.

Luck fluctuates in gambling. Sometimes you win, sometimes you lose. However, the goal for intelligent gamblers is to protect themselves in the times they lose and that means to set loss limits, not only for a particular session but for the long run as well.

EMOTIONS & SELF CONTROL

Smart gamblers have one thing in common—they know how to manage their money and keep cool in the thick of the wagering, whether they're up and riding high or struggling against a cold streak with the worst of luck. Superior playing skills alone does not make one a winning player. The concept here is self-control: the ability of a player to keep the game in check and never lose sight of the winning strategies.

Winning and losing streaks are a very real part of playing the lottery. It is how you deal with the inherent ups and downs at the games that determines just how well you will fare in the long run.

You're going to lose sometimes. You're also going to win sometimes. It is the smart gambler who will minimize losses when he's losing and not start betting wildly to chase past losses. It's all about emotional control. You can't change the numbers that will get drawn. You can, however, change your reactions to the results, and control the set of numbers you pick for the next drawing.

13

TAKING IT TO THE NEXT LEVEL

In this book, I have armed you with powerful strategies to attack lotto and lottery games with strong and fundamental tools. You've learned how to run analyses for all lotto and lottery games, plus the multi-state games like Powerball and Mega Millions. The various strategies that form the heart of your winning approach—Best Number, Overdue Number, Cluster, and Lucky Number Analysis—are Level I Strategies. These powerful strategies are the foundation for beating lotto and lottery games, and my Level II and Level III strategies are entirely dependent on this strong base.

As I wrote earlier, you will sometimes use *uneven* distribution of your chosen numbers by design, which will be taking you from the powerful Level I strategies detailed in this book to Level II and Level II strategies, material introduced in *Lottery Super System*, my more advanced book on beating lotto and lottery games. *Lottery Super System* is for players who are ready to graduate from even distribution of chosen numbers to strategies focusing on uneven distribution.

In *Lottery Super System*, you will learn how to identify and use keys, and how to combine Level I and Level II strategies into super powerful Level III strategies. You'll learn how to work with kings, queens, wizards, earls, dukes and courts, plus other advanced Level II keys to attack every major lotto and lottery game.

For players who want the most powerful strategies ever developed, the back of this book describes the most advanced

Level III strategies ever created. And for players who want to harness the power of an online computer strategy specifically designed for beating lotto and lottery games, the following chapter describes how to do just that with my online site, *www.lotterysupersystem.com.*

14

USING ONLINE SOFTWARE TO WIN

To harness the most powerful tools possible to beat lotto and lottery games, you want to use a computer program designed specifically for this purpose. There are so many variables, combinations, trends and numbers to track, and so many results to tally, especially if you are going to use advanced strategies, that software specifically designed for identifying and tracking patterns and past histories of lotto and lottery games gives you a big advantage over players who rely solely on old-fashioned traditional methods.

If you have been charting results by hand, I don't have to tell you about the tedium involved in this painstaking process. It's hard work. The good news: This is the computer age and with the help of a good program, you can obtain results in a matter of clicks, as opposed to a matter of hours or even days, depending upon what you're trying to accomplish.

It's like drawing water from a well and walking it a mile back home when all you have to do is turn on a faucet. With advanced strategies you still will have handwork, but with just a few clicks, the computer generates basic analyses upon which many strategies rely.

For example, if your strategy calls for a regression analysis of 100 or 250 games, discovering best numbers, cold numbers, clusters and all the various kinds of streaks and patterns would be an enormous task for just pen and paper, especially when you consider all the types of results you would like to obtain from the data.

Besides the difficulty of charting by hand, which is certainly a valid way to analyze games, it's a matter of the best use of your time. You are better off *analyzing* data rather than spending hours *compiling* it, and better served asking the computer to do certain things for you and then figuring out the best way to parse and use the results. If nothing else, you could concentrate your time on fine-tuning your strategic approach, interpreting and using the data in a more advantageous manner, or just spending time with other activities you enjoy.

You will still do a certain amount of hand figuring because the programs aren't set up for everything you need, but you'll have a really good helper by your side.

You need serious tools nowadays to attack lotto and lottery games. Luckily for you, there is the computer and *LotterySuperSystem.com*.

LOTTERY SUPER SYSTEM.COM

My online software program, *LotterySuperSystem.com*, automates the key Level I strategies and keeps track of just about every winning lotto and lottery result in the United States and some other jurisdictions. You can click on any state, from California and Oregon to Texas and Florida and all the states in between, and you'll get the winning results of every game played at whatever regression level you need. That's a tremendous amount of vital information available in one click. Imagine trying to find all those results and not knowing where to go, especially if it is a different game that you haven't been following?

That's why I created *LotterySuperSystem.com*. I had been creating designer strategies for serious lotto and lottery players for a long time. I also had been working on systems for casual players. Most of all, I loved to analyze the numbers and patterns and think of ways to beat lotto and lottery games. But no work could be done on lottery games by mathematicians like myself, or casual and serious players, without easy access to the results of past drawings that we all rely on.

I've designed *LotterySuperSystem.com* so that, within seconds, you can analyze hundreds of games back into lottery history. A set of powerful tools lets you customize your favorite lotto and lottery games and analyze numbers according to criteria you've established. The goal is to enhance your lottery experience, add hours of enjoyment to your day, and give you all the information you need to craft the best winning tickets possible. And then let luck take its course.

It's pretty easy to see what my program is all about. There is a free membership level and it allows you to access a lot of free information on lotto and lottery games, plus use some core strategies. Well, without further ado, I'll just say check it out and let *LotterySuperSystem.com* help you along the way to winning jackpots.

15

JACKPOT!

We've covered a lot of material in this book—how to extract and use chosen numbers, frequency analysis, positional analysis, wheeling strategies, lucky number analysis, and much more. Now it's time for you to put everything together and go for the big jackpot that can set you free.

You now know how to use the powerful Level I strategies that are the centerpiece of beating lotto and lottery games of all shapes and sizes. These powerful tools can be used to beat any lottery or lotto game in every U.S. state and Canadian province. They are also applicable to pretty much every lotto and lottery game offered in the world.

By following the strategies here, you can increase your chances of winning huge million and multimillion-dollar jackpots. Now you just need a little luck to go your way. If you play your strategies well and all the numbers fall right, one day you just might look at the winning numbers, and then look at them a second time in disbelief, and uncontrollably scream out what your eyes can barely believe:

Jackpot!

G

GLOSSARY

6/25 Game: A six-ball lotto game with a pool of 25 total balls from which six winning balls will be drawn.

6/49 Game: A six-ball lotto game with a pool of 49 total balls from which six winning balls will be drawn.

6/51 Game: A six-ball lotto game with a pool of 51 total balls from which six winning balls will be drawn.

6/54 Game: A six-ball lotto game with a pool of 54 total balls from which six winning balls will be drawn.

Abbreviated Wheeling System: See **wheel**.

Anchor Ball: The lowest numbered ball in a cluster.

Balls: The physical balls used in lottery games, each one designated with a number that, if drawn, is one of the winning numbers.

Best Number Analysis: A chart that draws on the raw information from a Positional Analysis or Frequency Analysis to identify numbers that have been the most frequently drawn over a specified number of games.

Best Number Frequency Analysis: A chart that sorts the data from a Refined Frequency Analysis Chart and sorts it from numbers most frequently drawn to least frequently drawn.

Best Number: A number that was drawn at a greater frequency than randomness would suggest. Also **hot number**.

Bias: A tendency of certain events to occur at a greater or lesser frequency than pure randomness would suggest.

Big Wheel: A pool of multiple players acting together as a syndicate to buy a block of tickets and share winning prizes.

Box Bet: A lottery ticket which wins if the three or four numbers chosen appear in any order—as opposed to a *straight ticket*.

Burst: A regression analysis of 10 games or less.

Chain Ball: The highest numbered ball in a cluster.

Chosen Numbers: Numbers a player has chosen, through any of the analysis methods or thorough sheer randomness, to play in a lottery or lotto game.

Cluster Analysis: The science of charting and statistically identifying and analyzing balls that have shown a tendency to be drawn together.

Clusters: Groups of numbers that have been drawn together in an individual drawing. Also called **paired numbers** or **paired groups**.

Cold Number: A number that was drawn at a lesser frequency than randomness would suggest. Also **Overdue Number**.

Combination Bet: In three-ball lottery, a bet on all six combinations possible for three chosen digits, in essence a six-ticket bet.

Core Strategies: The powerful everyday strategies players use to beat lotto and lottery games. Also called **Level I Strategies**.

Dual-Pool Game: A game that features two pools of numbers, typically one set from which five balls are drawn, and a second set from which one ball is drawn. Multi-state games such as Powerball and Mega Millions are dual-pool games.

Five-Ball Lotto Games: A lotto game with a pool, typically of from 25 to 54 balls, that draws five balls and awards the jackpot to the player or players who correctly choose all five numbers, and smaller prizes to players who correctly choose four, three and sometimes two of the drawn numbers.

Four-Ball Lottery: A lottery game that features drawings from which an individual ball will be drawn out of a pool of 10 balls, numbered 0 through 9, from four separate and distinct drawings. Players must pick the exact order of all balls drawn to win the jackpot. For example, if the draw is 0-3-7-5, the winning ticket must have those four numbers in exactly that order.

Frequency Analysis: The science of charting and statistically analyzing the winning balls in lotto games from a specified number of previous drawings.

Full Wheel: A wheeling system that includes every possible combination of chosen numbers, as opposed to an **abbreviated wheel** or simply, **wheel**.

Grouping: A group of two balls drawn together in a lottery or lotto game.

Hot Number: A number that is drawn at a greater frequency than randomness would suggest.

Instant Game: A lottery game with the results predetermined on the ticket so that after purchase the player can immediately verify whether he has won or lost. Also called a **scratch-off game**.

Jackpot: The very biggest money prize, signifying a huge amount of money, in a lottery or lotto game.

Key Numbers: The most important number or numbers among tickets played in a lottery or lotto game, ones that have a player's highest confidence and will get played more frequently than other chosen numbers.

Letter Conversion Chart: A chart that assigns one letter to each chosen number so that the chosen numbers can be correctly inserted into a wheel template.

Level I Strategies: Powerful everyday strategies such as best number, overdue, and cluster analyses, which are used to identify the top performing numbers in a series of past lotto and lottery drawings, and as a basis to make winning tickets. Also called **Core Analyses**.

Level II Strategies: Strategies that identify the most important chosen numbers—or bring in numbers from outside that group—and treat these numbers in a more aggressive or *more important* fashion when forming tickets.

Level III Strategies: Strategies that combine Level I core strategies and Level II key numbers—or combine other advanced methods—as centerpieces to form straightforward or intricate strategies designed to beat lotto and lottery games. One type of Level III Strategies is called the **Exotics**.

Little Lotto: Lotto games that draw from a smaller pool of balls, such as 36 or 39 (as opposed to a larger pool of balls such as 49), and pick five balls.

Lottery Wheel: A system of distributing chosen numbers that gives players partial or full coverage of all their possible combinations such that a group of tickets can be played at a reasonable cost, that is, much less than if every combination were played. Also called an **abbreviated wheeling system**.

Lottery: A game that features separate drawings, each containing 10 balls numbered from 0 through 9, from which an individual ball will be drawn. Players typically pay $1 per ticket to play and must choose the exact order of all balls drawn to win the jackpot.

LotterySuperSystem.com: A user-friendly online program specifically programmed to identify all winning lotto and lottery drawings over a long period of time and to use that information to create powerful and advanced winning strategies designed to beat future drawings.

Lotto: A game with a pool of balls that draws five or six balls and awards the big jackpot to the player or players who correctly choose all those numbers correctly, plus smaller prizes to players who correctly choose some of those winning numbers. Players typically pay $1 per ticket to play and may play as many tickets as they choose.

Lucky Analysis: An analysis that gives players the option of inputting their own lucky numbers into the tickets they play.

Lucky Number: Any number that a player feels is lucky for him or her and chooses to play as a chosen number or key.

Mega Millions: A large dual-pool hybrid lottery game offered in more than forty states that features two pools, one with white balls and one with gold balls, with the grand prize growing at times to hundreds of millions of dollars.

Money Management: A strategy used by players to preserve their capital, manage their wins, and avoid unnecessary risks and big losses.

Multi-state Game: A hybrid lottery game offered in multiple states that pools all the bets together to form a massive jackpot of prize money. Also called a **Dual-Pool** game.

Numbers: Any of the various balls, represented by numbers, in a pool of balls that have been drawn in lotto and lottery games, or that could be drawn.

Overdue Analysis: An analysis that refines data from Frequency Analysis or Positional Analysis charts that identifies numbers that have been the least frequently drawn over a specified number of games.

Overdue Frequency Analysis: A chart that sorts the data from a Raw Frequency Analysis Chart by order of frequency—the opposite of a Best Number Frequency Analysis—with the best performing number, that is, the most overdue (coldest) first, the second most overdue number second, and so on down to the hottest numbers.

Overdue Numbers: Numbers that have been the least frequently drawn over a specified number of games.

Paired Groups, Paired Numbers: See **Clusters.**

Pari-Mutuel Game: A game where the total amount bet, less money taken by the government for its fees and costs, gets placed in the prize pool.

Pick 3: A three-ball lottery game with fixed prizes.

Pick 4: A four-ball lottery game with fixed prizes.

Plays: Tickets purchased in a lottery or lotto game.

Position: The bin or drawing in lottery—first, second, third or fourth (if a four-ball game)—from which a ball is drawn. For example, in a three-ball game, first position indicates the bin from which the first ball is drawn or that it is the first drawing, second position indicates the bin or drawing from which the second ball is drawn, and third position represents the bin or drawing from which the third ball is drawn.

Positional Analysis Raw Chart: A worksheet of raw data for lottery games that keeps track of the frequency of drawings for each ball by position.

Positional Analysis Refined Chart: A chart that translates the dots in a Positional Analysis Raw Chart into numbers such that the frequency of drawings for each digit in a lottery over a specified regression level can be determined at a glance.

Positional Analysis: The science of charting and statistically identifying and analyzing balls *by position* from a specified number of previous lottery games in which each ball gets drawn from a different bin or drawing.

Positional Drawing History: A chart that shows the date of drawing and the balls selected for each drawing, by position, over a specified number of lottery drawings.

Powerball: A large dual-pool hybrid lottery game offered in more than forty states that features two pools, one with white balls and one with red balls, with the grand prize growing at times to hundreds of millions of dollars. Also, the name of the ball drawn from the red pool.

Raw Frequency Analysis Chart: A chart that displays the frequency of winning lotto balls from a specified number of previous drawings.

Regression Analysis: An analysis over a specified number of prior lottery or lotto drawings.

Regression Level: A specified number of prior lottery or lotto drawings,

Repeating Clusters: Two numbers that get drawn together in two or more drawings over a specified number of games.

Scratch-off Tickets: A lottery game featuring instant results in which the user scratches off a covering on a paper ticket to determine if he has won a set prize amount.

Six-Ball Lotto: A lotto game with a pool, typically of from 25 to 54 balls, that draws six balls and awards the big jackpot to the player or players who correctly choose all six numbers, and smaller prizes to players who correctly choose five, four, three and sometimes two of the drawn numbers.

Straight Bet: In lottery games, a bet to pick the winning number in the *exact order* drawn.

Straight/Box Bet: In lottery games, a bet that the ticket played comes in exactly as picked or in any order (a straight bet plus a box bet) as long as it contains the correct numbers drawn. (This is actually a two-ticket play.)

Three-Ball Lottery: A lottery game that features drawings from which an individual ball will be drawn out of a pool of 10 balls, numbered 0 through 9, from three separate and distinct drawings. Players must pick the exact order of all balls drawn to win the jackpot. For example, if the draw is 2-9-0, the winning ticket must have those three numbers in exactly that order.

Ticket: A slip of paper representing a bet on a lottery or lotto game.

Wheel Template: A template that matches letters of a wheeling system with a player's chosen numbers so that wheels with good coverage of these numbers are created.

Wheel: A system of strategically distributing chosen numbers that gives a player partial coverage of all possible combinations such that a group of tickets can be played at a reasonable cost.

Wheeling System: See **Wheel.**

LEVEL III LOTTO WHEELS
50% OFF!!!

The advanced **Level III lotto wheel packages** are specifically designed to work with the advanced Level III strategies in the colored papers' series. They feature one-key, two-key and three-key wheels in a variety of combinations—from 7-18 chosen-number combinations and purchases of 5-25 tickets—and are built to give you optimum coverage of Level III chosen numbers and power keys extracted from the Level III strategies.

These **professional-level lotto wheels** are formulated for players looking to optimize their chosen numbers coverage with the goal of hitting huge, monster jackpots!

Level III Emerald Lotto 6-Ball Wheel Package
50 Powerful 6-Ball Wheels $50, Just $24.95!

The emerald package includes 50 professional 6-ball wheels covering a variety of your chosen number, ticket purchase, and key packages as described above.

Level III Diamond Lotto 6-Ball Wheel Package
100 Powerful 6-Ball Wheels $100, Just $49.95!

The diamond package includes 100 professional 6-ball wheels covering a variety of your chosen number, ticket purchase, and key packages as described above.

Level III Sapphire Lotto 5-Ball Wheel Package
50 Powerful 5-Ball Wheels $50, Just $24.95!

The sapphire package includes 50 professional 5-ball wheels covering a variety of your chosen number, ticket purchase, and key packages as described above.

Level III Ruby Lotto Wheel Package
100 Powerful 5-Ball Wheels $100, Just $49.95!

The ruby package includes 100 pro 5-ball wheels with a bank of chosen number, ticket, and key packages, plus a section with wheels for super aggressive players and syndicates (10-20 chosen numbers, 20-100 tickets) seeking jackpots worth $100s of millions.

Level III Treasure of Jewels
Emerald, Diamond, Sapphire, Ruby—$300, Just $150—now $124.95!!!

All the jewels together—Emerald, Diamond, Sapphire, Ruby—for **50% off** $300. Now just $150! Reduced $25 again! **$175 OFF** total for readers of this book!!! Only $124.95!

Master Lotto and Lottery Strategies
-Prof. Jones' Winning Methods For Non-Computer Users-

Now, for the **first time** anywhere, learn Prof. Jones' **exclusive** Lotto and Lottery advanced **winning** systems. This package is chock-full of **powerful information** designed to give you an edge like never before!

It's time to play the Lotto and Lottery like a **pro** using Prof. Jones latest **scientific winning** systems.

Look at what you get -

50 WHEELING SYSTEMS

That's right, **50** advanced Dimitrov Wheeling Systems! You'll be playing with the most powerful lotto and lottery winning systems ever designed. These brilliant and revolutionary **winning systems** can be used successfully by anyone!

FREE AUTOMATIC WHEELING TEMPLATE AND INSTRUCTION GUIDE

Prof. Jones' **exclusive** automatic reusable plastic wheeling template is **included free** with your package and allows you to automatically record winning numbers. Also included is a specially written instruction guide that shows you how to use the wheeling systems and the templates provided.

Spend **only several minutes a day** inputting past winning numbers into the master templates and this **amazing system** quickly and **scientifically** generates the numbers that have the **best chances** of making you rich.

BONUS AND EXTRA BONUS!

Order now and receive 10 master Positional Analysis templates **and** 10 master Frequency Analysis templates, **absolutely free** with your order!

To order, send $24.95 by check or money order to:
Cardoza Publishing, P.O. Box 98115, Las Vegas, NV 89193

FIVE BALL LOTTO WHEELS
Prof. Jones' Winning Strategy for Non-Computer Users

SPECIAL 5-BALL STRATEGY PACKAGE

For **5-ball lotto players**, this special package **gives you the master strategy** five ball wheels that allow you to play your **best numbers** and go for the big wins that other players dream about! **Popular and powerful**, these wheels get you ready for the action.

30 WHEELS INCLUDED

A **wide variety of wheels** covers bets for all situations, from **5 game plays** with a variety of best numbers, to wheels covering **24 game plays**, and others covering more than 20 of best number picks.

You'll find wheels such as 7 numbers-12 plays (7/12), 11/3, 19/18, 6/6 and 25 more great wheeling combinations to cover all your needs.

OTHER FEATURES

The 5-Ball Lotto Wheels Strategy Kit also contains **20** 5-Ball Lotto Sum Templates, a **clear Template** for ease-of-use in wheeling your best numbers, and a **5-Ball Lotto Sum chart** to provide a range of numbers and a guide in number-choosing strategies to help you win.

BONUS - Wheeling instructions included!

To order, send $25 by check or money order to: **Cardoza Publishing**